What We Talk About
when we Talk About It

Variations on the Theme of Love

Edited By
Susannah Carlson
&
Shelley Valdez

VOLUME
2

*What We Talk About
When We Talk About It*
Volume Two

*Edited by
Susannah Carlson and Shelley Valdez*

Table of Contents

TABLE OF CONTENTS

In Tenderness and Faith

Emerson Tenney

She sleeps in her bed this night. Her mother's bed. The bed has white linen sheets on it, and she likes the way they feel against her skin. There is something about linen that she could never quite get her head around—it was rough and not, sometimes it made her look fashionable, and other times, like she'd just escaped a cult, and like anything good and everyone she loved, it wrinkled easily.

She doesn't ever wear clothes to bed. This may have started on the night of nights. After it was over, she drove back to her mother's loft downtown, where she lived, and bled, briefly, into the porcelain toilet, staining the water rose, before stretching her long, white body across her sheets until she felt the skin pull over her ribs, pores cracking. She slept like that. Like the first time and not, because this time she could be alone with herself. This was perhaps only the second time she'd thought she was more than a daughter. "I am a woman," she hears resounding across the space between her ears. She stretches further into this new warmth. Why ever change, after? She did not.

Many, many nights had sewn themselves between then and this night she sleeps in her mother's bed. On that night, she fell asleep quickly, and on this night, quickly too. She is on the brink of returning—to the other end of the country, to college, to a life that is both now and becoming. She imagines she is enfolded in one hundred layers of fabric. They grow heavy around her, pushing her down into one hundred more layers of fabric underneath her. These underneath layers push her up with the geological force of the Earth's molten core, while the atmosphere pushes her down. She is buoyed between, naked, and forgets everything.

Her mother lies next to her, a pillow between them. A great distance. She wants to read off her iPad, maybe play online poker, but she remembers her daughter tries to avoid digital light sources thirty minutes before going to bed. She puts her phone face down on the nightstand and flips onto her back. She stares up at the ceiling in the dark. She can hear her daughter breathing. Though she does not turn to look at her, she can feel the way her daughter shifts onto her side, facing the window, facing away from her, and the small mmm that slips out of her throat when she lands in that comfortable spot and lets the day leave her. She thinks about her daughter's bare skin under the linen, the comfort and ease with which she leans into necessity, sleep. My daughter is more animal than me, she thinks, and she is overcome with jealousy.

At night, she can never cover herself enough. Her daughter laughed at her once when she zipped a sweatshirt over her pajamas before getting into bed. "It's like you're getting ready to go to the store."

The mother felt this a challenge. "I like to be warm when I sleep," she said. What she did not say was that she wore a full pair of underwear beneath her pajama bottoms, and socks. This started, the mother thinks, when she was eight and had worms. She had to sleep in her nightgown with no underwear, so her mother could sneak into her room in the night and lift up the nightgown to look in her bottom with a flashlight. This surprised the worms, and her mother could see if she had them. The mother falls asleep thinking about this, with visions of great worms writhing across the ceiling and her daughter beside her.

The daughter wakes to the sound of coughing. She can see through the curtains the moonlight, and everything else dark. A few cars, a distant police siren, and are those crickets? The sounds tell her it is still time to be asleep. It must be two or three in the morning, she thinks. She follows the coughing to the bathroom. There she finds her mother shaking. The mother sits curled on the bathmat in her pajamas and shakes while hot water runs into the bathtub. She approaches her mother cautiously. "Mom?" she asks aloud. The mother coughs. "Mom, are you alright?" She kneels beside her mother on the white mat and places one hand on her quivering shoulder. When her mother looks at her, she sees that she is crying. The sound of the running water burbles as it hits the steaming tub. They sit a long time, silently. The sound of running water. Eventually, she helps her mother out of her pajamas, leaving them on the floor. The mother steps over the rim of the bath. She sinks into the rising steam. The daughter remembers the word balm. She hopes the hot water may be as much.

But the coughing does not stop. Instead it intensifies. It grows longer and rougher, more ragged. The daughter is caught in between. On the one hand she wants to give her mother privacy, she is, after all, naked, coughing in clear bathwater, but on the other hand, she does not want to miss anything, anything critical, important. Also, it is hard to look. She settles on an in between—she keeps her eyeline just over the rim of the tub, hovering between the bathwater and her mother's thigh. She thinks they should go to the doctor. She thinks the bathroom might be shaking. They should go to a doctor. Something is wrong. And then suddenly, the bathwater is turning pink. The daughter looks up and sees her mother is coughing up blood. The blood drips down her chin like mashed raspberries. The bath is roses.

They are getting in the car. They are driving very fast, even though the mother says not to. Even though the mother says she will be alright, the daughter does not believe her even though she wants to. They barrel onto the CA-110 South. The daughter puts in a CD, Simon and Garfunkel. Good for anything. She looks over her shoulder and changes lanes. Keeps left to merge onto the I-10 West. She keeps left. The freeway is black. Very few cars. They get off at Olympic, slight right onto San Vicente.

The mother groans, "I don't feel good."

"I know, I know." More street. Stop sign. "I promise we are almost there."

And then they are there. Cedars-Sinai Medical Center opens out in a sprawling plaza, but the daughter makes a right before they reach it and pulls into the valet.

"Hi, yes. We're checking in."

She takes the ticket. It is pink like roses.

The mother cannot stand at the check-in counter, so the daughter looks through her purse for her mother's ID. She forgot to tell her mother to bring her wallet. She forgot you needed to bring your wallet to the emergency room. She learns other people have forgotten this before too. "It is not necessary now."

The mother is in a bed and they are wheeling her away. She looks at her daughter growing smaller at the end of the hall as she moves backward into space. In the fluorescence, she cannot tell whether it is day or night. The walls she passes are shades of pale yellow and white. The floor looks like linoleum, but it is hard to tell. In her daughter's grandparents' home, they had linoleum flooring in the kitchen. That is where I learned to cook, she thinks. That is where I taught myself. The mother remembers her father's black shoes on the linoleum and his hand, worn and wide, when he handed her a quarter for the first dinner she ever cooked for her family. She was nine. The bed shakes, stops. The mother feels like she is falling, or floating. They are in the elevator. I have never been in an elevator while I was lying down, she says, but no one hears her. Then they are out of the elevator and rolling again. It is smoother now. Maybe this room is carpeted. The overhead lights flick. Hushed tones mingle with the taps of shoes around the rolling bed. The mother feels a prick in her right arm. Then everything is white, and it is like moving backward into eternity.

Eternity ends for the daughter at 4:32 am when the nurse comes out and says her mother is in room 5421. "That's the fifth floor, and then you make a right. You can't miss it." The room is behind two doors. Each door is marked by the same sign. The daughter heeds neither. Inside the room, the curtain is lifted, and the window stares out into the thick, black space of parking lot asphalt. In the distance, on Beverly Boulevard, a few streetlights steep in eerie blue haze. She turns to face her mother, who will not know she is turning to face her, not yet, but maybe soon.

Her mother lies face up on the hospital bed. There is a tube running out of her mouth, running its way down along the side of the hospital bed and into a machine. The daughter cannot name what exactly the tube does, other than signal severity. She walks over to the bedside and stares into her mother's face. What she wants to say is that tomorrow morning they will wake up and her mother will get out of the bed and they will walk down to Beverly Boulevard, where the furniture shops cluster together, and they will play the future apartment game, naming all the pieces of furniture they will put in their future apartment; maybe this time the apartment will be in London, or New York City, and they will decorate the spacious rooms until lunchtime when they will walk down Third St. to Toast Café, and order matching tuna melts and eat them in the sun, where things are alright. This is what the daughter wants to tell her mother.

Instead she looks at her face, quiet and somber in the looking ahead kind of way. She looks down to her mother's chest. A great hole gapes between her mother's collarbone and navel. It is dark and deep.

The daughter places her right hand lightly on her mother's left arm and leans toward her. She leans toward the hole, until her head is inside the gape in her mother's chest. The daughter blinks. Inside it is darkness, but not blackness. The dark is deep navy. When the daughter blinks again she sees that there are pinheads of light in the dark. Stars. They shimmer and flicker against the deep. The daughter wants to lean in farther, but to do so would be to let go of her mother's arm. She stays like this, clutching her mother, half out of the world and beholding the universe.

Induction
Lisa Dordal

Of course I asked first. Raised as I was
to be good. What's one glass? you said.
At fourteen, surrounded by a spirit
I took for love. Everything hard
softening. The way your own mother
tucked bottles of bourbon
into the folds of your freshly laundered clothes
sent home, during college, for washing.

Two weeks later, my own festive six-pack.
Five brightly sealed bottles on the table,
next to the ornamental angels spinning
round and round from the heat of candles
below. The sixth at my lips: my left fingers
clasping its slender neck, as if it were
a tin whistle. My right hand resting delicately
on the bottle's dark, glassy body. You, next to me,
lovely as ever in your long, green Christmas dress,
hair freshly set, face perfect and bright—
looking straight at me. Smiling. Can you see

why I shuddered when Father's new wife
ordered your drink? "Manhattan"
slipping from her mouth. As though
it was that which he loved, wedded himself to:
the taste on your lips, then hers.
"Manhattan" hovering in the air between us
like some sweet angel of you,
returned.

It's Hard to Cheat on Your Husband
with Your Mother-in-law
Living Two Doors Down

Amanda Moore

But Pam's trying her hardest, subterfuge
part of the seduction. Who can blame her? She's young,
not twenty six: three kids, two dogs
    who churn her yard to mud,
a dozen empty bottles haunting every room, her husband's
boots on the floor all day like a threat.
So I don't say a word
when she sends her lovers, all scrawny limbs
and tank tops, baseball caps and black tattoos,
out the back door and across my yard
to the cars they leave huddled on the side street
bulky and obvious like awkward kids in gym class
just hoping to be ignored. I appreciate
the wide berth her paramours
give the blocks of light my windows cast
across their path, the way
they don't even glance
between the curtains. I hardly know they pass
but for the rustle of soft steps in grass, a curl
of smoke scent through the open window,
blaze of ember streaking the dark.

Your Sweet Voice Calling

Flo Golod

Happiness is unhinging Frances.

In the evenings, alone, when her new lover is off doing whatever lovers do when they're not attending to love, her reading is disturbed by a sly insistent tickle that erupts into a demanding host of sensations, thrilling and upsetting. When desire floods her, she feels stupid and malleable. Will her entire life structure of useful hard work and self-improvement collapse? She frets that she's becoming lazy and foolish.

Frances now shuts her office door. She doesn't want anyone to catch her smiling stupidly at no one. When a receptionist places her on hold, pouring pop music into her helpless ear, she passes the moments licking her lips, tenderly reclaiming kisses from the night before.

Her workouts have been rigorous propitiations to the destructive powers of middle age, but love generates renewed enthusiasm for her body. Now she exercises with the same attention and vanity her neighbor devotes to his 1954 Chevy. They both look good.

She and her lover prepare extravagant meals, chopping, talking, kissing, and tasting. Ravenous, she then finds herself full, almost without eating. Hours later, after love, she stalks the kitchen for leftovers. Her lover is bemused by all of this. He is a person so openhearted that a condition couldn't be considered, let alone placed, on his love.

This drives Frances crazy. She tries to find the door that won't open. She argues about politics, musical taste, whether or not to keep dogs in the city. Her lover debates her with energy but no apparent stake in winning. He listens willingly to any music Frances plays, even the abstract, irritable jazz she favors.

Frances rarely sleeps, making her edgy, pale, and easily distracted. She wonders if love makes her sick. She gets a cold. When cold sores deface her mouth, her lover deftly deposits kisses on other body parts, letting her besieged lips heal without denying her love.

Her lover is a naturalist. He knows trees, flowers, shrubs, and grasses. She knows only rose, daisy, maple, and fern. She is grateful for green things but has no curiosity about their nature. When they walk down the street, he greets each shrub, tree, and flower. The music of her lover's voice harmonizes with the world around them, as he names what grows and tells her bits of lore about each. Frances will remember almost none of this, but his descriptions comfort her. She feels like an identified plant. Glossy, blooming, named, and understood.

Frances reads her lover a poem full of plant names. He smiles and nods. He tells her that he likes poetry but often feels overpowered in the face of its condensed dreamy demands. He had a lover who was a poet. Frances immediately wishes that she could find this woman, wrench the pen from her hand, then wreck her computer with a Luddite's hammer. Frances decides she will not read her lover any more poems with plants or trees in them. She switches from jazz to the gentle ballads he favors. She finds this music sentimental, but she is not as opposed to sentiment these days.

One day her lover says he wants to visit his horse. He keeps a horse in the country, boarded by a woman who was once his lover. Would Frances like to visit, meet the horse, Mildred, and the former lover whose name also starts with an 'M'? Frances doesn't want to appear as small and grudging as she feels so she agrees to meet horse and woman. She confesses her fear of horses. Her lover promises to introduce them carefully. Frances believes him, but she feels foolish. The prospect of trembling before the horse, while she is watched by her lover and her ex-lover, makes Frances apprehensive.

Her lover and his old flame are casual and direct with each other. Frances likes this woman, and they talk about books and politics while he takes a ride on Mildred. When he returns, the horse is tired. He introduces her to Frances. Cautiously, she holds out an apple. The horse's wet, velvety lips tickle her palm as the creature takes the offering. They take the ex-lover Molly out to dinner, then drive home in the dark, reminiscing about long rides in the country when they were kids, and planning a trip they might take together.

That night Frances dreams that the horse is gently nibbling her shoulder. Her sleeping body does not resist.

Her lover's name is John, the most generic male name. She thinks of him only as her lover. She realizes this is strange. She calls him John, but in reverie, he remains her lover. She doesn't like to talk about him. She fears he will become less her lover, and more John, a specific figure in the world. Once released, she might lose him. She prefers the slightly mythical state of their relations and accepts the strain on her friendships as she holds back the usual details of connection and conflict that women talk about when they talk about men.

The first time Francis becomes truly angry with her lover is when he leaves her for a week. He's been invited on a naturalists' outing to identify and classify things that grow in an Alabama swamp. Environmentalists want the swamp protected by the federal government. It is worthwhile but sudden, and Frances is stunned by how long the week seems.

Before her lover turned up, Frances tended her life alone with a gardener's careful patience and some fatalism about weather conditions. Now that single stoic life looks small and pot-bound, a windowbox instead of a tropical forest. Frances is furious that her old life doesn't satisfy when her lover is gone. She is terrified that he will disappear into an Alabama swamp, or into the arms of a compatible naturalist who will whisper the names of growing things in his ear. She defended her old life so steadfastly. Could that old life again be all she has, and will she lose faith with it?

Frances is stricken. Love has made her dependent.

When her lover returns, Frances talks about her last lover, a scoundrel. She describes a car trip where they broke down in the north woods and she stayed in a locked car while he hitchhiked to the nearest town, failing to return, and forcing her to hitch her own ride. Her new lover frowns and asks careful questions.

"You had a time of it with him, I guess."

He tells her that she can talk about her ex if she needs to. He is glad to hear her stories, to know her better. Frances feels ashamed of herself. She wasn't telling stories about her ex in order to be known better. She was trying to get a rise out of him. She wonders if anything makes this man angry or jealous. She asks and he says,

"Frances, I used to hit people."

Frances wishes she hadn't asked. Her lover knows he has frightened her.

"It doesn't happen anymore."

She remembers stories he has told her about a brutal father and a hardscrabble country life. She'd always thought of him as a miraculous ascendant out of a harmful past. It never occurred to her that her lover had to stumble roughly through decades of adult life to become his gentle self.

For a time, Frances is uneasy. Anyone's past produces some bitterness, trouble that can't be tamed or denied. Since her lover rests so comfortably in the life he lives, the one she's begun to share, she cannot understand that it was ever otherwise. Could this loving time be merely a mild season, followed inevitably by hard weather?

Frances goes away for a few days and sits on the Lake Superior shore, watching the rocks and big waves she loves, wondering why now they signify such terror.

She returns and, of course, her lover is glad to see her. They cook, eat, tell stories, and walk through a park, where musicians busk for dollars. Saxophones and violins thicken the twilight with a longing that lifts her heart in an arc, triumphing over doubt.

Later, they make love in rhythms the music made from love and for all the lovers who loved before them. Patterns of flesh and sweat flicker in candlelight. He invents names of flowers and grants them absurd functions, planting them with his tongue in her navel. They laugh until a playful kiss deepens and tightens her shaking belly. The urgent force of sex makes them greedy and quiet. Later, somewhere between the luscious surprise of climax and the slippery fall to sleep, Frances startles awake, terrified.

Her lover rouses. "Are you alright?" She murmurs a reassurance and he slides away from her, back into his own dreams.

Frances knows this love will drive her into another life. Whatever comes next hovers dreamily but won't form a shape. Whatever comes next can't be imagined alone. It requires two.

Frances falls asleep and dreams of John.

Postcards I Wish I'd Sent Lisbeth
When We Were Girls
And Her Parents Sent Her Away

Jackie Craven

July 8, 1962

The afternoon heats up like an engine.
It revs up the vapor hill,
rips through Mrs. Dooley's hollyhocks,
roars your name with gasoline breath,
and then, at the top of Forsythia Lane,
flops onto Mrs. Emery's lawn,
panting *Lisbeth, Lis—*

July 11, 1962

Don't confuse this gasping day
with the ragged dog Mrs. Emery keeps
tied to her Virgin Mary. He's a sundial
in the grass, spinning silly circles,
yowling at the Good Humor man
who jingles past. Zingos and Lollies
dissolve on my summer tongue.

July 23, 1962

When will you return?
The plaster Virgin sings to me,
but her voice is sugar rough.
The singular vessel of devotion
can't hold our secret words.
Grownup faces peer through
thirsty windows. *Quick,*
stop the truck. Jackie needs a
black cow float.

August 5, 1962

Again today, I hear ice cream toll.
Time turns somersaults over rooftops,

Mrs. Dooley's peonies flutter off
on smoky wings. You melt over the rim
of my frosted cone. Soon you'll fling
your arms around some flea-bitten
boy. You'll forget our special language.

August 19, 1962

Isbethlay,
omecay omehay.
Isbethlay,
arrymay emay.
Marry me forever.

October 12, 1962

Summer is dropping from the hickory tree.
You're a husk carried off by squirrels.
Even Mrs. Emery's dog has forgotten you.
Go ahead, ask him who he loves.
He'll only bark his name:
Ralph! Ralph!

The Prophet Bathes In Styx
Sage

join the cicadas to sing at the sun
& mourn the moonlight each dawn
every dawn in america goes like this:
      i get scared in the night
     by sounds outside my window
     i can only attribute to the cars
      that pull into my driveway
       to pull a U-ie

i've been driving the wrong direction
  most of my life. most of my life's been
   towards a kind of rage i can't explain

  a str8 boy raises his fist
  again
    & again the tremor in my chest
     frightens its way through bone
      into my skin

  a str8 boy raises his fist
  the only language he knows
  he speaks into my skin
  sweet words
  with his knuckles

    when cicadas are ready to mate
     they emerge from underground
     undead & unloved until
     they can find each other

Sage

part of me wants to go back to boy
part of me wants to give up this current self
we are at least three ways at once
& none of them intersect but they all touch

somewhere in the middle

is it enough to start with
an idea of how to live &
say that's enough for you
or that's enough for me. please
baby, learn to love me again

in Oakland a parade pursues the past
i stand in the streets covered
with con men dragging pennies from
    our pockets & blaming capitalism

alright, i say, i hear you
    but do you have to take my bread?

some crumbs mean patience
some crumbs mean prophecy
Hansel & Gretel left a trail for
Tiresias to find them in the woods
blind prophet sniffing in the dark
i wanted to tell my father about
    all the girls i'd never bring home

he wants me to find love
but i've been looking
in the wrong places   maybe a parade is what i need
                             maybe some pride & true

tried on you for size & of course
you fit like a second lid sliding
over my golden eye blinded by
the dazzle of divine Tiresias wanted foresight of the future
so for his sight Zeus granted his wish

"Let the prophet bathe in Lethe / That his prophecies be
                              mark'd as memory"

when i imagine us together
i can't help thinking
i'll have to give up something too

Zugzwang
MeeRee Orlandini

I am reading this online article about moves
And she's comparing our two art forms:
poetry to chess, I am pissed.
I was trying not to see you:
You are not on this walk with me up Passyunk Ave.
You are not in the prepared food section of the grocery store.
You are not at the Barclay sipping cocktails
         with chess moms.
I am hurt by this accusation:
 "There are an infinite number of possible games,
but experienced players know the classic openings
        and defenses."
You tried to teach me once in the park
so I ate the bishop and the rook and tucked the board
under my arm like a newspaper, screamed
Checkmate! Checkmate! Checkmate!
until you calmed me down.

Kairoi

Dennis Mombauer

Outside the hotel, European flags flapped in the breeze. The man crossed the hall, suit on his shoulders and shoes banging on marble. He knew he could always adopt the easy arrogance of privilege, the confident stride of the white western male.

The woman sat in the lobby corner, her nails clicking away on the laptop. Work deadlines, work calls, work trips. Nothing came to her, everything had to be taken: against her skin, her gender, her heritage.

The man stopped in front of the woman. She finished her sentence, saved the file, and looked up at him.

They kissed.

not

Sharon L. Charde

spin or dazzle, stars
exploding, no,
more like a kitchen
counter, the sharp knife
that slices summer
tomatoes, the bird feeders
you've set up at every
window that spill seed
all over the winter snow.
It's the car that always starts,
the messy woodstove, its firelight,
your garden sprouting ragged
kale, arugula and beets.
We will survive you said
when our son died and
I had no idea how we'd
mow the lawn or shop.
It's your hand on my back,
our late afternoon walk,
the second world we have
to inhabit.

After the Fight

by Jenn Richter

She strips the corn of its husks
and tassels, plunges it into the roiling
pot on the back burner.
The lid clatters to the floor.
She kicks it aside, narrowly missing
the old Collie, who slinks to his rug
in front of the long-extinguished fire.

She slaps the salmon into the pan,
slices the surface so it can better absorb
a quick drizzle of olive oil and spice.
She shoves it beneath the broiler

and turns to the stash of kale—
regal green rimming purple like a fresh bruise –
chops it once, twice,
tosses it into the simmering skillet,
to be seasoned only with sea salt
and a splash of fresh lemon.

She calls the kids. They stomp across the sagging
porch. The screen door slams
against the sill as they maneuver half-naked bodies
into chairs still sticky from breakfast.

They glance at the empty space
at the head of the table
and bow their heads to say grace.

End
Emily Rapp Black

And you wouldn't know it,
Watching the father now, his face
shielded, a dark hood for this
medieval disease, leaning over
the body of our boy, hand that once
touched you, made math: him and you three,
holding the perfect
foot no longer warm but doughy, alight.

The father holds the boy's body down, slip of paper,
the white shroud so careful,
heavier than all his wasted bones combined,
and you wouldn't believe that
this father would grow teeth
in that moment of goodbye,
that he would open his mouth, lean over and bite,
killing every good thing.

Separation

Kat Hausler

Though it was hours past midnight, Manfred was suffocating in the sealed tram. He forced himself to count his breaths. It had been a summer like a splash of oil in a hot pan—sudden, overwhelming heat, sure to burn off just as soon. The car Manfred was sitting in was empty but for two androgynous teenagers, kissing and groping with black-painted fingers, and a bum, an icon of drunkenness enshrined in empty bottles in the seat across the aisle. None of them looked as uncomfortable as Manfred felt.

This was the last tram tonight and Manfred had hurried to catch it, not because of Lydia's nagging, but because it would be inconvenient to find a taxi or walk home.

He had planned to stay out all night and thus avoid his wife, but Lydia would only have gone into hysterics whenever he came in. She never went out anymore, so there was no hope of slipping in unnoticed. She would weep and ask when he'd stopped loving her and why he'd married her just to treat her like this. But that wasn't the reason he was coming home now. He didn't care what Lydia said, and it was already too late to avoid upsetting her. There just hadn't been anywhere else he felt like spending the night.

The tram stopped and the two teenagers exited without disentangling themselves. Probably off for some unprotected sex, Manfred thought. He had little nostalgia for his own youth, which had been spent largely on now-irrelevant military training—five years pledging allegiance to the socialist fatherland, and in the end you better not write on your resume that you had served, not in that army. When the closing doors stirred the air in the tram, a wave of dried sweat, beer, and unwashed hair broke over Manfred. He gave an accusing look to the only other remaining passenger, but the bum was too far gone to notice, or too used to it to mind. Manfred felt disgusted. Didn't he have any self-control? Take Manfred, for example: He had drunk steadily all evening and even now remained aware of his surroundings. Not that Lydia saw a difference—to her, Manfred was just another bum on the last Friday night tram.

Lydia's mother had left her drunk of a father when Lydia was five, so for her, anyone who had a few drinks to relax after work was an alcoholic. She even talked slowly when Manfred came home nights, as if he was too plastered to understand. He could have strangled her sometimes.

The tram stopped and a squadron of tourists got on, stretching a map like a parachute between them. Manfred was sure they were going the wrong way—there was nothing out here, least of all hotels—but decided not to say anything.

The next stop was Manfred's. He wondered whether the bum ever left the tram or whether he sat in the same stupor day and night, leaving only to panhandle for fresh beer. After the salt-sour air in the tram, even the still, humid night was a relief. If there had been a breeze, Manfred told himself—and if he'd been coming home to a different woman—he might have enjoyed the few cobblestoned blocks to his building. As it was, his thoughts sloshed from one extreme to another as he tried to guess how Lydia would attack him when he came in: would it be cold, suspicious questions tonight, or would she scream at him for ruining her life?

And yet, however desperate their straits, Manfred and Lydia had never had a serious talk about divorce. Divorce was a threat made in the heat of the moment—by Lydia while storming out, or by Manfred, shouting after her from the doorway. There had always been a lot of that, even back when things were okay. Lydia was more melodramatic than she'd seemed while they were dating, and had a way of packing up over the least trifle. But between the fights, he and Lydia had managed to forget how hateful they both could be.

Coming home to her had made work bearable. She could turn the dull hours of his day into amusing anecdotes just by listening with a crooked smile and mischief in her eyes. Lydia worked from home and kept the apartment tidy—more than a refuge, it had been a place of elevation, a peak to which Manfred struggled all day to ascend. Everything had been light with Lydia, as if the problems of life outside their home were a running joke between the two of them. How well Manfred could remember all that—and yet he no longer felt lifted by her presence. Now he was plagued by what had once rescued him, and he sought escape elsewhere—escape from Lydia's sobs and the crime of not being able to make her happy, escape from his own distrust. Once he had hated himself for bringing her to tears; now he hated himself for not believing in her sorrow. Did Lydia ever cry when he wasn't looking?

Manfred unlocked his front door and began to tiptoe upstairs—for the neighbors, not for Lydia. He'd spoiled her too much at the beginning; that was it. Everybody had said he spoiled his girl. Even Lydia had said so. Now she expected too much.

That, and Manfred had lost respect for his wife. If she'd been flaky all along, at least she'd been strong. Decisive, ready to leave. Now she was a soft, teary thing that could barely stand to live. The more Lydia accused him of not loving her, the less he cared for her, and the more she claimed he wanted to leave, the more he did. A simple formula, and yet one she could never get the hang of.

What a waste, all of it. Manfred had once or twice considered leaving Lydia for a young, slightly overweight office assistant whom he sometimes met for drinks and a quickie, but shit, what a waste. Not just the years, but Lydia herself: her long, laughing eyes and slender limbs, the languid western dialect she spoke with her family, adding a long row of Ns to his name: Mannnfred. It could have, it should have, turned out okay. She was a few years younger and had been considered a catch—a woman no one notices when she comes into a party, but who knows how to put a smile on every face in the room. Only now she had stopped smiling. Manfred couldn't say what had happened, when their fights stopped being brief intermissions in their happiness and took over the stage.

The apartment was darker and more silent than the side street Manfred had just left, and it might have been a sepulcher for all the greeting he got coming in. Great, Manfred thought. She's doing the thing. The pretending-to-be-asleep thing. So she can pretend to get woken up, and bitch about how inconsiderate he was, and how late. Lydia had seen a doctor for her so-called insomnia, but Manfred didn't believe a word of it—no matter which pills they prescribed her, his wife would still lie in wait, ready to abandon the guise of sleep the moment he came in. Manfred switched on the overhead, and sure enough the bedroom door was closed, no light beneath it. He imagined the relief he would have felt entering an empty apartment, and for the first time, it occurred to him that this was a real possibility.

It was simple. He would wake Lydia, and she would be angry. Instead of apologizing, he would let the fight build. Neither he nor Lydia's pride would give in, and she would leave. All this had happened before. The difference was that he wouldn't let her come back this time.

Why had he never thought of this? Manfred stood in the middle of the living room, staring at the white rectangle of the bedroom door. So simple, yet something held him back, some nagging suspicion: What was the catch? If it were really so simple, wouldn't he have done it by now?

Manfred looked around the room, as if there might be some visible trap set in it. In the kitchenette, the doors of the yellow china cabinet were hanging open—Lydia knew he hated that, hated her thousand ways of leaving things half-done, hated all that had once endeared her to him. He wondered whether she'd done it on purpose, and glanced to the opposite wall of the room, to see whether Lydia had put bedding on the stiff velveteen sofa to indicate he should sleep there—but she hadn't, and Manfred turned back to the kitchen. He would slam the cabinet doors and it would be her fault if that woke her, her fault for leaving them open.

But a small white paper caught Manfred's eye on the dark expanse of the kitchen table—one of his wife's famous notes. If he'd held onto all of them, he'd have had an encyclopedia by now. Once they'd been senseless bursts of affection, scribbled on the backs of receipts. Lately, they were pages of passive aggression and hinted-at accusations: 'Don't know where you are…' 'Would have been nice to see you…' 'Have a good night anyway, wherever you are'. He crossed the room in three long steps and picked up the paper.

There wasn't much on it and the few words were dark and thin, lost as frail blackbirds in a heavy snow. Without malice, without deceit or manipulation, Lydia reminded Manfred how madly, how tenderly they had once loved one another, and thanked him for their time together. The last line was a farewell.

Manfred stared at the dark forms flitting across the page and did not understand what his wife was trying to tell him. He smoothed the paper onto the tabletop and tried to force the restless flock of words to sit still. Images of Lydia settled in his mind, then took flight as if startled by the approach of new thoughts. Just last week she had said, 'I would put a gun in my mouth if I thought it would get a reaction out of you'.

He tried to recall the day before—had they fought? Had they been unhappy—enough for this? But the day was a handful of sand tossed onto the seaside, impossible to recollect.

Had he made a mistake? Perhaps Lydia had only left him. Manfred read the note again and felt more helpless than ever in his life, helpless because Lydia had abandoned not him but herself, and with this paper in his hands, there was nothing more to hope for. Would the neighbors have heard the gunshot, would someone have called the police? He would call them himself. He would call for an ambulance, the firemen, and all the people in this city who couldn't make his wife whole again, couldn't patch together the pieces of her broken mind. He couldn't picture the gun parting her half-smile, couldn't believe the laugher would die out of her eyes—not forever. And yet he had to call for the help that could not help them anymore.

Manfred went to the sofa and picked up the cordless phone from the side table, and then the breath went out of him, and he sat on the edge of a velveteen cushion, listening for a dial tone. He pressed one once, and then again, then hung up the phone—they would ask him questions. They would need details. One way or another, Manfred had to get himself into the bedroom.

I am going to stand up, Manfred told himself. I am going to stand up and go through that door and know for certain my wife is dead. He said this again and again in ten seconds that lasted longer than his whole life, but the ache in his gut was so deep and heavy, Manfred was sure he himself was dying. He could barely move for the pain. Oh, Lydia!

The wings of her image still fluttered through his mind as he stood up, but he could not lay hands on a single one of them: Her laugh, bright and sudden as a splash of yellow paint—he could not capture its sound. Her way of relating absolutely ordinary information in a thrilling whisper—but the sound of her voice flew off and left his ears aching with the sudden blast of silence. On his journey across the room that lasted as long as his marriage, Manfred recalled teal-colored eyes through damp clumps of lashes, Lydia's nails digging into the flesh of her arm when she couldn't bear something, and her way of biting the round knuckle of her thumb to stifle a sob. But trying to build his wife out of these memories was like trying to construct an eagle on the basis of a stray feather lying in mud.

His hand on the doorknob, Manfred felt his ribs heave, as when, in the grip of some childhood flu, he'd vomited out the contents of his stomach, but been unable to stop gagging and shuddering. The last traces of Lydia took flight, and Manfred's longing for her was a barren field where the dry grass still trembled from the flapping of vanished wings. The shadow of a memory passed over him, filling him with a cool, gentle peace, and he wanted to speak aloud to it, call it by his wife's name. But the shadow dispersed, and hot sobs burned into Manfred's throat and remained caught, choking him. He was terrified. Even Lydia's nagging, even her screaming at him to get out of the apartment, would have been precious solace in this wasteland of silence.

Something broke in Manfred, and he pushed open the bedroom door. Though he shuddered at what he must see—her lovely face gone, her fiery blood clotting on a pillowcase, no eyes either to reproach, or to pardon him, and her slender body so still—Manfred forced himself to switch on the light. Before the police came, he would kiss whatever remained of Lydia goodbye, and if God were merciful—Lydia, at least, had always believed that—somewhere some immortal piece of her must know his agony.

Manfred turned toward the bed and his heart stopped as his wife raised her head a few centimeters from the pillow, and gave him a drowsy smile. The pieces settled into place again, lovely and whole. He couldn't recall the last time he had seen Lydia so peaceful.

"Oh, you awful…" Manfred tried to sound as if he'd taken it all as a harmless prank, but the sobs had gotten free now and wouldn't stop tearing their way out of him. He switched off the light and left the phone by the door, because he and Lydia didn't need to be saved by anyone but each other. Taking off his shoes and jacket, Manfred tumbled into bed and pressed himself to the curve of his wife's back, wept into Lydia's soft copper hair, kissed and clutched at her to make sure she was real, alive.

"I'm so sorry," she murmured, and the words were slurred with sleep. "It was a nasty trick to play on us." The bottle the apothecary had given her sat on the nightstand, and Manfred was relieved that Lydia hadn't sat up waiting for him, after all. The new medicine would help her to a good night's sleep, unplagued by recent sorrows, and they would wake together, refreshed and ready to start again. It had all been a kind of nightmare, but they were going to wake from it for good.

"No, I'm sorry," Manfred insisted, kissing Lydia's cool, smooth hand. "Oh, darling, can you forgive me?"

But Lydia had already drifted away to her dreams. Manfred lay awake awhile, his heart glowing with hope. He ached with tenderness and adoration for the woman beside him, as he had carrying her through his doorway after their wedding. His life was blessed with Lydia in it, and Manfred realized now the depths of despair he would have sunk to without her. Falling asleep with Lydia in his arms, he was a man resurrected.

It was almost noon the next day when, sitting up to stir Lydia from her heavy sleep, Manfred noticed the way the late morning sunlight shone through the translucent bottle on the nightstand, unimpeded by contents. And although Manfred had been ready to believe in all manner of fairytales the night before, no amount of his tears could restore sight to Lydia's eyes this morning, and even his most fervent kisses could not wake her.

How to Be Alive
Ryan Havely

Say she sleeps
while you work
but your work
doesn't mean much
and her sleep
keeps both of you
alive. Say you know
beauty when you see it
but can't find the words
to tell about it later.
Say you leave
a window open in the rain
or find a mitten floating in a creek.
Say something hateful
to somebody you love
and apologize. Say something
you don't mean
to somebody you don't love
and harbor the guilt
until you die. Say something
nice, to somebody, and think
it must be true. Say life
is pretty good sometimes.
Love somebody
and other people, too. Carve
your initials in a park bench
or a tree or float them
down a river.
Help where you can.
Tap somebody on the shoulder.
Say you went to Woodstock.
Get sad because somewhere
somebody you don't know

is alone and about to die,
or get sad because somebody
you know is as alone
as the rest of us.
Give the cat
a little bit of your pizza
and laugh and laugh and laugh.
Start a joke you never finish.
Notice even the clouds
that don't look like anything,
and hope that once you were loved.

In The Dust

Erika Rasmussen

There is solidarity,
those little particles
every bit as much of you
as the hands that usher
them away with a rag.

That is where I want
to be, humble, accumulating
on every surface, emerging
with greater fury each time

      swept away,
      because the air can't be
      caught and it is

all but natural to fall
      in love with the things
that touch us, that we reach out
to as if they are
      home.

The German Credit

Sylvia Maultash Warsh

Quite unexpectedly that spring, the family next door to Herr Kalb sold their house and moved out. The next few weeks the house remained empty but for a couple with two teenaged children who visited regularly after supper. Through the window it was always the same: the tired parents coaxing cartons out of the car, the fat girl and her brother careening over the untended lawn.

Herr Kalb often stayed inside on their arrival, though he would have liked to go out and work in his garden. He avoided interaction. It wasn't worth forcing oneself to be civil to cretins. Who could tell what kind of people they were, to have a daughter as fat as that?

His two-bedroom house faced a seldom travelled street. It was like the far end of a rabbit warren, a self-enclosed curve from which there was no exit. There were never any children or animals, never anyone sitting on a porch. It was the kind of street people lived around the corner from for years and never saw. The kind of street Herr Kalb had been looking for half his life. Its squared-away neatness appealed to his sense of order and somehow reminded him of the English, whom he had always admired for their reticence. He liked to think that here, he was surrounded by reserved English families who would be too shy to ask any questions. Indeed, after six years of living on the street, he knew his neighbors on either side only to nod at.

One Saturday, the quiet morning drew him out of his house into the garden. Wearing the shiny leather boots again made him feel strong and nostalgic as he crouched to pull some weeds out of the soil. He enjoyed pulling them out by the roots, he hunted for them not just around his flowers but in the lawn as well. Instead of spraying them with weed killer, like other people, he went along his property, carefully examining the grass for foreign leaves, for buttercup, for clover. With a sharp knifelike tool to cut deep into the earth, he loosened the soil around each offending clump and pulled slowly, almost gently, always with a thrilled heart, to get each thread of root. He knew how to do things thoroughly, he had always done his job right. If he was told to pull, he pulled; if he was told to kill, he killed.

Too late, he saw the car ease into the driveway, the family get out. He tried to continue what he was doing but found himself only going through the motions. He felt all eyes on him, as if he'd been caught strangling a bird. A shriek made him turn, finally: the younger boy led his fat sister in a frenzied chase toward where he kneeled amid his bushes.

Despite his chagrin, he was able to see she was a slovenly pig of a girl with great, round breasts that bobbed beneath an oversized blouse. Brother and sister were close enough for him to note the porcine quality of her thick pink lips and upturned nose. He imagined her eating large quantities of goose liver and the borders of fat on cuts of meat he hadn't allowed himself to eat for years.

———————

On noticing him, they stop. Beverly Rosen is touched by the little man trying to hide in his bushes. She straightens out her blouse and gives him her best profile, ignoring him the way women are supposed to when they find someone staring. His attention surprises and flatters her. At school, she is ignored relentlessly because of her weight. In the dark of her solitary nights she has dared to hope that there would finally appear a man who could see the real girl beneath the flesh. But he is so shy, people with depth are always shy. She can tell he is a well of deep feelings by the way he listens as her father introduces himself and explains their move as part of the drift of the middle-class population to the suburbs.

Beverly observes him sideways from her good profile. He is a curious creature in those leather boots. Pathetic looking, actually, with that narrow, stubbly head. And is he really blushing that awful purple color like a wound? No, it seems to be his natural color if one could call it natural. Such a man would not be easy to love but she knows how effortless it is to become accustomed to things, even her own vulgar image in the mirror.

Beverly is pleased to learn she will recognize at least one face in her new school. A teacher, Herr Kalb, has been mentioned in passing by one of the other neighbors, not quite so taciturn. He is a mystery on the street, it seems, keeping to himself studiously. That's probably all it is, Beverly thinks: studious. Sensitive people have to keep to themselves because those around them, no matter how well meaning, are able to inflict psychic wounds without effort. Herr Kalb is a man who has been hurt, she is sure, and is no longer willing to chance the pain again. She understands his silence; she shares it. People are blinded by the excess flesh on her body; they refuse to view the beauty beneath, the sensitivity, the luminosity. If only people were not so narrow, if perhaps someone could be found who was slightly off center to conventional standards of taste.

Herr Kalb marched by the military-green lockers in the hallway without a glance at the students to whom he taught German and who, he noted with pleasure, abruptly ceased all movement at his passing. Later, he knew they would smile obliquely at the swinging arms, the straight, straight back. But he made sure their amusement had an edge to it, a guillotine edge he would have liked the use of when he felt them noting his tubular-shaped head covered with dark patches of fuzz, or the ruddy skin that rose beneath, a complexion stoked by fires so faithfully tended it was always on the point of conflagration.

The life of the mind is all! he screamed at them through his eyes. *Despise the body and worship only what you know, forget hockey, forget rock-n-roll, read Nietzsche, read the philosophers, you Canadians are obsessed with hockey and Elvis Presley, you will always be less than dignified, you will always be… Canadian.*

Her Kalb, arriving in Toronto several years after the war, had always been the hub of rumors. It was a wheel he watched closely: he was a double agent who had been in the Gestapo and now worked for Canadian Intelligence; he was a resistance fighter who had won medals; he was a Nazi who had somehow escaped. Though more than fifteen years had passed, the stories multiplied in the absence of any apparent Mrs. Kalb or any family or even friends.

Herr Kalb didn't care what they thought; they were just guessing. Nobody really knew. A witness would have to come upon him by chance, he had not been important enough to seek out for himself. And it was a big country, you could get lost in a country like this that stretched from one ocean to another. He often meditated on this as he drove from his suburban bungalow to the high school where he taught classes of incredibly ignorant students the intricacies of the pure Tongue, the only comfort he had left.

Though languages defy her intuitive approach to learning, Beverly decides to take German to trouble herself further with the presence of the purplish, stiff-necked man who intrigues and repulses her at the same time. He has an unnerving habit of looking out the window, then naming an unsuspecting student as he swings his compact body around without changing the position of his feet. She may be the only one in the class who dares breathe because, from the start, she senses he will not ask her any questions. She knows he will not make her a victim.

While other students leaf with agitation through their books for answers, Beverly lowers her head respectfully, allowing herself chance moments to glance at his face, the stubble that is his hair. When their eyes meet, seldom enough, she feels her pulse jump. She is, perhaps, the only person who knows his face well enough to run her fingers over his features in her sleep. She has amused herself by drawing sketches of his face. Though neither the school nor her parents think much of it, Beverly's talent for drawing is the only thing she likes about herself. Her subject lately is limited to Herr Kalb. If she could sketch his portrait to pass her course, it would make more sense to her because as it is, she knows no German. But she knows, as does he, that he will not fail her; that somehow, no matter what she doesn't learn, Beverly Rosen will finish that class with a credit.

Thousands of faces filled his sleep, tens of thousands. Beverly Rosen's was there among the multitude. What did she want from him? Why did she stare so? She was too young to remember him, but the fat pig of a girl saw it in his face, every day she stared with those empty eyes, and she saw. He felt her sharp nails peeling layers of his skin, each class a new layer, he dreaded the hour each day, felt her nails on his face as she pulled. One day he would fall bleeding to the floor.

What was it she wanted? Revenge for her people? One would think they would want to forget, but Jews' memories were long. They still remembered when Moses split the sea for them but where was Moses twenty years ago when they needed him? A myth like all the others they had. They waited for a Messiah to rescue them (he laughed an infrequent laugh), he had been their Messiah, saving them the further pain of living by granting them the mercy of death.

It was his turn at lunch duty that day. He noticed Beverly Rosen staring at him between bites of a nauseatingly fatty corned beef sandwich. It was unbearable enough in the class, but out in the open like this! He felt a crack in his self-control that threatened to split up the middle.

From then on, he always found her watching. He was not prepared to be found out, not by this fat Jewish girl. But she couldn't remember 1942, the beards shaven, the shootings in the streets. Had he shaven the forelocks of her grandfather, her uncle? Maybe it was Papa Rosen, had he seen him shoot that boy who had smuggled a potato into the ghetto? They had orders, no food, there was to be no food. That meant no potato, it was all quite clear, but Rosen wouldn't understand that, and this fat, ugly daughter of his, who ate only fat, he saw the kind of garbage she ate, white cream-filled cakes, and meat laced with fat. His diet had dwindled to vegetables and fruits, some nuts. Even eggs were unbearable to him now. But Beverly Rosen grew round on what he couldn't eat.

On one of the last sunny days in September, Beverly finds herself setting up her chaise to face Herr Kalb's lawn despite the fact that in this position she gains no benefit from the sun, which rises behind. And though she longs to sustain the tan on her face, acquired over the summer, she finds it hard to resist this curious desire to watch her Teutonic neighbor creep out shyly to work in his garden.

Her pencil works constantly over the paper. She already has a series of sketches of Herr Kalb stooping in his garden, most of them hurried poses since he rarely stays long once he finds her watching. One, however, she manages to finish from memory, a profile shot with his knee on the ground and a tool in his hand, scooping the earth. She toys with the idea of signing it and dropping it in his mailbox. A harmless enough offering. It might begin a new level of communication.

Ah, there he is, marching round the front, armed with oversized garden shears and white gloves. He pretends not to notice her; she calls it diffidence. Wearing his high leather boots, he halts before the rose vines Beverly has admired during the summer. Blood-red, the flowers have climbed up the side wall of his house opposite her bedroom and, though distanced by a driveway, their perfume has often drifted on the morning air and into her shallow dreams, which break like bubbles on awakening.

While she watches, he crouches over the now-faded flowers, and with elbows jerking at ruthless angles to his body, clips the vines down to within several inches of the ground. White gloves maneuver the clumsy boughs into a bag. If the gardener ever felt the pain of any thorns, he doesn't show it. Beverly feels more ambivalent toward him at that moment than ever. But in the waning September sun, and with the increasing prospect of winter, she reluctantly reminds herself that she will not be loved by the football players of the school, nor the expert dancers, nor those who spend their free time in the French club. She decides to drop the sketch in his mailbox when it is dark.

There she was again, that stupid stupid girl. It had occurred to him to stay inside, waiting in his boots and gloves, but he knew he would be wasting his time, that she wouldn't go away. She was waiting for him. He knew she wasn't in his class to learn German; that any German she knew was purely coincidental. So there had to be another motive for her presence in his room. Even in the cafeteria, there was no escape. The constant confrontation with this globular apparition put him on edge. He was sure that round fat cells coursed through her blood, forming a kind of chicken soup. He wondered how long it would be before she told him what she really wanted.

One morning, in his mailbox, he found a very competent pencil drawing of himself burying something in the ground. It was signed B. Rosen. So it began, her campaign of molestation. He had been right. But he hadn't expected anything this frank. Here it was, and he was as open to attack as if he were standing in the middle of a field in the line of fire.

Beverly Rosen is embarrassed but gratified to find Herr Kalb glancing at her more often. In class his eyes will fall on her and at times stare thoughtfully. Sometimes she finds him watching her eat in the lunchroom. There is an unspoken bond between them that makes her feel closer to him than to anyone else. But she senses this resistance of his, this ingrained shyness that has built a fence around him similar to the one around herself. She longs to make a rent in the defenses wide enough for them to reach through and touch.

Herr Kalb searched his memory for Mr. Rosen, trying to pry from unexamined recesses a face that, at that time, must have been twenty. But they all looked alike with their heads shaven, the striped uniform. And his English, without a trace of accent. How had he eradicated that tell-tale Jewish lisp? But Rosen was clever, sending his fat daughter after him. The cow-eyes followed him everywhere, soured his digestion. His own helplessness rankled him till finally, out of defiance, he began to seek her out, face her on her own terms. But the toll was high, his dreams were full of her: Beverly pointing, Beverly eating, Beverly regurgitating. One morning he whipped himself into a frenzy while dreaming she chased him downhill into a pit. He woke up sweating in his sheets, and with the instinct of a wounded animal, headed for his mailbox. There he found another pencil sketch of himself, this time holding a knife at a murderous angle.

He knew this was the end. A few years ago, they had caught up with Eichmann; they rooted him out, manipulated him away from his home with their secret spy ring. They knew how to do these things, they were masters of deception. But would they waste their intrigue on such a small fish as he? Did they care so much about the few people he had disposed of here and there along the way? Were there forty? were there sixty? He had done his duty, he would reply.

He lost much sleep worrying about Beverly. He knew she was an agent, if not for her father then for others. These Jews, you never knew what traps they had in mind. Even in the camps, they watched him incessantly, waiting for him to act. But he had always won. Perhaps they had started these little fires in his brain purposely, hoping they would erupt into an inferno that would consume him. Yes, that was it, they were trying to destroy his mind. But he would keep one step ahead of them, that was the advantage of superior brainpower. They wanted to play their stupid cat and mouse games; they would find out who was the cat and who the mouse.

———————

Beverly Rosen can't be more surprised to see Herr Kalb at her front door. She only vaguely hears what he is saying because the blood thundering past her ears blocks most of the sound. The sketch has worked. Sometimes one needs only to reach out. She is prepared to show him her considerable collection of sketches, thinks of the mess her room is in, when she realizes he has raised his voice. The typewriter, he has said quite vehemently. Could he use the typewriter while his is being repaired?

She steps aside, bewildered, and leads him to the dining room, where she types her homework assignments. In an uncomprehending stupor she pulls the case onto the table, unlatches it, and lifts the cover. As she exposes the typewriter thus, she feels, herself, uncovered. A perplexing shame overtakes her, that her unabashed thoughts have brought them this far. And the embarrassment she feels for him is acute: that he has resorted to such a deception to come to her. Will she have to deliver a sketch each time she wants some personal contact with him? She will draw endlessly.

After ten minutes at the typewriter, he leaves without ceremony. Her disappointment abates when, on removing the typewriter again, Beverly discovers a piece of paper he has left behind, a cryptic love note. What depth, she sighs, what unknowable depth. In the middle of the stark white page: "As you see, I am not afraid of you."

———

During the weekend, Herr Kalb found another sketch of himself in the mailbox, this time of his face with all its irregularities, his fuzzy hair. Looking for clues, he was horrified to find a note printed neatly across the bottom of the backside of the page: "It's always hard to expose oneself and admit to the truth. We try to hide our real selves, the side we don't want others to see. But it all comes out in the end. Tomorrow my mother is preparing a batch of chopped liver for the weekend. I will deliver a container of it to you and try to persuade you that hiding behind a mask is not the answer. I have captured you in this sketch, but it is not enough. As you see I am not afraid of you either. Bev. R."

———

Though the end of the year, it is a lovely beginning to things. Beverly lifts her face expectantly to a crisp blue sky as she crosses the lawn.

She climbs the steps of her neighbor's front porch, bearing her container of chopped liver. Through the glass stormdoor, she can see the front door is open. She knocks on the glass but there is no answer. She welcomes the chance to enter the beloved house, and steps in. Herr Kalb, she lilts, keeping the bowl before her like an offering. As she moves forward, a sudden shadow fills the door. She doesn't comprehend it but recognizes the sun as it glints off the weeding tool that Herr Kalb stabs down into the chopped liver. It splashes to the floor. Beverly fails to notice the polished leather boots and above all, the brightness of Herr Kalb's eyes, as she leaps out the door.

He Wanted His Ashes Scattered in Ireland
Kathleen Hayes Phillips

and in easier times, we talked
about the how's and when's of such a trip,
the possibility of such a journey.

We remembered our travels,
the places we loved,
ourselves, younger and full of future,
forgetting why we started the conversation,
but glad we did.

When he died, it seemed so easy.
It seemed he planned the timing, the airfare,
even the place to stay—

All I did was pay attention
and follow his directions,
traveling in the first person singular,

but never alone.

Lost & Found in The Universe

Carolyn Martin

It starts upstairs.
Have you seen my leather gloves?
Could have been her credit card, underwear,
the photos of the Maui beach we left
our tensions on. Whatever can get lost,
does – every day of every week.
I can hear you roll your eyes! she adds.

It drives her up a wall – that adolescent look –
so I sort of lie, returning to the files
I'm scrolling through downstairs.

I'm in love with scientists who scour
galaxies and bring their mysteries
down to earth. The sun rings *like a bell*,
they claim. Black matter's like a *paperweight;*
the universe, a captive *butterfly.*
And here's this *lonely cyan gem*
hanging out with *cool brown dwarfs;*
there, a *planet-killing star*
running from a *cosmic crime.*

While we, in two-thousand-plus square feet,
can't unearth bank receipts or scrubbing pads
we swore we stored beneath the sink.
We can't remember where we hid Christmas gifts
or what we thought we bought and when. Or …

Never mind. I found … thumps down the stairs.
She's waving her black gloves, an earring lost
last spring, the mail misplaced two weeks ago.
This will be her next triumphant theme:
She'll find what she's not looking for.

I counter with one crafted line –
Found is found in any space – and offer her
a galaxy gourmandized by scientists
from Bonn. Its center, so they claim, tastes
like raspberries and smells like rum.

Retired Speed Freak Chopper Rider

Jesse Sensibar

Nobody knows it but you weep at the drop of a hat. You weep holding your five-year-old nephew to your chest. The tears stream down your hardpan face. You go to the movies alone so you can cry silently in the dark to yourself. You think to yourself that without knowing it you may have reached the maximum level of pain one can absorb in a single lifetime, that now to absorb any more you must release some, but you cannot simply empty that deep swimming pool of hurt, sorrow, and regret all at once, cannot pump it out of the pool and across the yard into a Tucson gutter like a minor flashflood of regret. No, you can only cry it out one tear at a time like single drops of water evaporating off of the desert at dawn. You will cry at any provocation, all your life you worked to feel nothing, like a desert, and now like a desert in spring, you cannot stop feeling everything. Sometimes you speak of what you have done and what you have not done, what you have not felt and feel, and you begin to weep silently as you talk. You cannot control it. The tears squeeze out one drop at a time like bleeding. And you could laugh without a sound at yourself, watching yourself, feeling yourself, feeling yourself feel completely alone, and you laugh because you know that finally you are wrong, finally you are not alone. And you hold that five-year-old child to your chest like the desert in bloom, and you weep silently but finally.

Anachronisms
Bryan Shawn Wang

The tree asked, "Who dares enter the Forest of Antiquity?"

Hennie's son looked away. These days, Corey was always look-ing away, as if he couldn't engage with anything or anyone aside from his new friend—the friend who now was regarding the tree person with a cruel smirk. Hennie felt sorry for the actor, having to maintain his gravitas while facing the boys' apathy and disdain, while smothered in green and brown body paint and cloaked in artificial shrubbery.

"Corey," Hennie called, pulling her phone from her purse. "Let me take your picture with the forest fellow."

"Are you kidding?" Corey muttered.

"For the scrapbook." Although Hennie hadn't gotten to her scrapbooking table in months. Although she was still working through pictures from first grade. Someday she'd catch up—crop and stamp her way through Corey's childhood until she was back in step with him.

"I don't do photos," said the friend, Parker. "My parents won't sign model releases. It's a matter of principle."

"Model releases?"

Parker shrugged. "Sorry, Hennie."

Hennie didn't mind Parker's addressing her by her first name. When Corey was small, she'd had all of his playmates (back then, Corey had had plenty of playmates) call her Miss Hennie, even as the other mothers—Mrs. Jones, Mrs. Bollinger, Dr. Guterson— insisted on more proper forms of address. Hennie was the young, hip mom, the one who crouched when she talked to the children and didn't feel it in her back, the one who scampered up the jungle gym with ease, who could teleport at will to make believe worlds. She was a distressed fairytale damsel, a misunderstood ogress, an alien visitor seeking a peaceful home on Earth. She didn't mind.

Indeed, heard as an echo of those days, Parker now calling her Hennie was a kindness, however unintentional.

The tree person was scowling now, but his belligerence was unconvincing. "You have an elaborate costume," Hennie told him. She rapped her knuckles against his trunk. "Very, um, hard."

The tree's scowl vanished. "Art thou hitting on me, Hennie?"

Hennie blushed. "Excuse me?"

"Don't be shy," the man said in a gentler voice, his coaxing tone almost effeminate. Beneath the tangle of leaves and twigs that served as facial hair, he smiled. "Come here and hug a tree. I think my sap's starting to run."

"Why are you saying these things?" Hennie asked. Tourists were beginning to stop. Corey and Parker edged away, and she wondered how much they'd overheard, if they thought she'd hit on the man, if they knew what it meant to hit on somebody. She turned and started off, trying to put the tree guy and his innuendo and antiquated forest behind her.

"Wait, Hennie," the man called, but Hennie hurried after her son.

Reaching the boys, she said, "He was a little forward, wasn't he? That—what do you call it? Dryad? I thought forest folk were generally timid."

"Dryads are female," Parker said. "Were you flirting with a girl?"

Corey looked disgusted. "It was an ent, Mom. You know, from Middle-earth?"

"China?" Hennie had taken a class on Asian cultures in college, but she'd spent the lectures daydreaming about her unmarried professor, a young British chap—keeping the man's house, which would be one of those cozy, unpresuming cottages on the north side of campus; reading bedtime stories to their self-assured and immaculate children; accompanying him to the other side of the world to tour sites of minor historical significance in Japan, the Koreas, the Middle Kingdom.

"Middle-earth." Parker's smirk reappeared. "You haven't read Tolkien."

Of course, she'd read Tolkien. But that was twenty-five years ago.

The path took them past Legacy Forge, purveyor of fine weapons and armour. As Hennie followed the boys into the shoppe, she wondered if re-reading Tolkien, sharing in Corey's latest sideline, would make her a better mother. Would, for instance, dressing like an elf dispel his stubborn aura of sullen disfavor? She pictured a petite, more slender version of herself in form-fitting earth tones, endowed with large, shapely ears. She grimaced. Probably the only thing that would accomplish would be to turn her husband on.

Behind the counter of Legacy Forge, a stern, balding man in a leather apron brandished a blacksmith's hammer and a Diet Coke. The boys headed for an imposing display of finely honed metal.

"This halberd is so boss," Corey said, running his fingers along a massive weapon, part battle axe and part bayonet. "Mom, will you buy this? Please? I'll be your friend forever."

Hennie tried to make a joke of it. "I'm afraid you might put somebody's eye out."

"That's the point," Parker said. "Get it? Point?"

"Touché," said Corey.

Hennie decided that there was nothing more obnoxious than a pair of thirteen-year-old geeks who'd recently discovered wordplay. Although no sooner had the thought begun to stick than she tried to unthink it. She hated when her husband applied any label even remotely disparaging to their son, and she often accused him of having lost all of the compassion his Christian upbringing had bestowed on him. (Although he'd lost not a smidge of the conservatism.)

"They need to keep their hands to themselves," said the shopkeeper. He tapped a sign that read, *Thou Breakest It, Thou Boughtest It*. Corey had his hands around the hilt of a broadsword. Parker had his hands around Corey's wrists, trying to wrest the blade from him.

The man asked Hennie, "Are you planning to buy anything, or are you just going to let them keep fondling my hardware?"

"I'm sorry," Hennie said. "Although your merchandise doesn't appear particularly fragile."

"I don't like stray fingerprints on my weaponry."

"Then ask them to stop. You can treat them like adults."

"You want me to treat them like adults?" The man stepped around the counter.

Hennie hesitated. Of course, Corey and Parker weren't adults. They were barely teens, wickedly sharp one minute and oblivious the next, alternately transparent and aggravatingly inscrutable. And no matter how independent he believed himself, Corey still needed his mother.

"Come along, boys." She made her voice bright, as if she were diverting a pair of frisky, overcurious puppies. "It's time to move on." Miraculously, the puppies obeyed.

"What an asshole," Parker said, when they got outside.

"Utter," Corey said.

Hennie frowned. "I don't like that word."

"Utter?" Corey asked. "Or asshole?"

"The second one."

"But it's accurate," Parker said. "It's authentic."

Corey said, "Speaking of authentic, did you see the guy's wristwatch?"

"Now that's an anachronism." Parker laughed. "Spock five." He raised his hand in a Vulcan salute, which Corey returned. The boys jammed their hands together, fingers still spread—a gesture Hennie found vaguely obscene.

"I don't think we should stoop to criticizing the man's outfit," she said.

"His garb, Hennie."

"His garb. He was protecting his business. Understandably. Let's not dwell on it. Let's try to enjoy the day."

Parker looked at Corey, and Corey looked at Parker, and Hennie burned as she felt the stigma of supreme lameness applied to her. She was the mother tagging along, lagging behind, hobbled by her ignorance and misplaced enthusiasm.

Nevertheless, she trooped on, exclaiming over a jester on a unicycle, a glassblower drawing out an alchemist's flask, a chainsaw artist carving a glaring dwarf from a tree stump. But her cheery docent's demeanor steadily wilted before the boys' searing indifference. Bored. She'd driven them fifty miles, spent nearly a hundred dollars getting them into this Faire, and they were bored. She could imagine her husband's reaction when she told him about it: simultaneously peeved and smug. Tyler had always refused to cater to Corey. (Which meant Hennie was forever mediating between them. And failing: nowadays, it seemed she no longer stood between her husband and her son but rather found herself at a remove equally distant from both.)

Hennie didn't completely trust the boys on their own, but searching for a way to salvage the outing, she asked, "Would you like to wander by yourselves for a while?"

Corey and Parker instantly lightened.

"Yes, please," Corey said.

Parker, claiming he was absolutely famished, requested coinage for victuals. Hennie reluctantly handed each boy a twenty, and they swaggered away, easy and suddenly erect. She could have smacked them. If they'd wanted so desperately to get rid of her, Hennie thought, they should have been the ones paying to split up.

She turned away, trying to collect herself, trying to remain gracious and grounded, to want what she already had.

A barrage of laughter drew her attention. A gang of boisterous actors had ambushed some faire-goers with their bawdy banter. Avoiding them, Hennie pretended to inspect the wares in the window of a shoppe called Talismans & Trinkets. A trio of fiddlers strolled past, their bejeweled garments winking at her in the sunlight, their jaunty air spurring her back into motion. The atmosphere, she thought, was indefatigably festive, and if this collective nostalgia seemed a bit silly—this nostalgia for an age that preceded them all by centuries, for an age that maybe never was—at the same time, the underlying desire for a wholly different era almost made sense to Hennie. She could almost understand her son and his pompous little friend.

Ten years ago, no one would have questioned Corey's fascination with all things medieval. Hennie recalled a morning at Story Hour, the children's librarian reading from a picture book adaptation of Sir Gawain and the Green Knight and then having the children construct cardboard shields and swords. Ordinarily, Hennie reveled in Story Hour, the community of mothers taking time out from their chores and errands, the care of their suburban knights and castles (although naturally they all fully appreciated their storybook lives). On that morning, however, Corey had wanted absolutely no part of knights or castles, chivalry or combat.

Which made his recent interest all the more, well, interesting.

Although interesting wasn't exactly how his father would describe it. A few weeks ago, when Corey had asked to accompany Parker to a local meeting of the SCA, Tyler said, "The Society for Creative Anachronism? Those freaks who put on Elizabethan dresses and suits of armor and spend their weekends dipping candles and strumming lutes?" Tyler had no use for the creative or the anachronistic. He was only social as long as it could help him close a deal.

"It's a hobby, Dad."

"You're too young for a hobby. And too poor. You can get a hobby once you get a job."

Hennie had refrained from inquiring whether the same edict applied to her.

Even though Corey's foray into the realms of fantasy puzzled Hennie, she'd suggested this expedition to the Renaissance Faire as a compromise. Now that she was here, however, seeing all of these grown men and women in costume, assuming imaginary personae—she couldn't help recalling the denizens of her college dormitory's sub-basement, those feral geniuses and near-dropouts so intent on their Dungeons & Dragons campaigns that they rarely surfaced mid-semester. Their defiant nonconformity had intimidated her. Did Corey share that aversion toward reality? Hennie wanted a son who was content with his world. She wanted a son who was still content with her.

She stood before The Flaming Flagon. Already, at two in the afternoon, the establishment hummed with thirsty tourists. Hennie slipped into a tiny booth at the back of the bar.

The ale was bitter, warm, and expensive. Hennie forced a sip down and surveyed the crowd. These were people, she imagined, looking to ditch their children, or their spouses, or their lives. People who had been ditched.

A rotund man in a plumed hat, pantaloons, and a cape approached. "What ails thee, gentle lady?" He held the half-chewed leg of some unfortunate bird in one hand; in the other, an oversized tankard.

He squatted awkwardly beside Hennie. "Prithee, sweet maiden, quoth me thy troubles." He cocked his head dramatically. His mustache was flecked with grease and bits of drumstick, and he was heavily perfumed.

Hennie shook her head. "Please. I'd like to be left alone."

"Alone?" The man chuckled. "Who visits the Faire to be alone?" He set his cup down and extended his hand. "Come, milady. Mine is not ordinary company."

She shook her head again. Not alone. Although once upon a time she truly had wanted to be alone—or at least divested of her infant son, who'd wanted to nurse every other hour around the clock, and of her husband, who'd still bothered her in the bedroom. She'd yearned for one single night alone, a night in which she could keep her sore and swollen tits all to herself.

But she'd wanted a family, too. And somehow she'd grown accustomed to not being alone.

Not that she was interested in the fat man's attention. "If solitude art thy desire," he was saying, "mayhap the Faire itself be thy obstacle? If happiness, however, then mayhap thy own self?"

"Mayhap mine obstacle," Hennie said, "be the corpulent figure with archaic speech and questionable hygiene who invadeth my personal space?"

The man, with some difficulty, stood. "Thou woundeth me, wench."

Hennie returned to her lousy beer as the man lumbered off to badger another patron, a tall, younger woman whom he strenuously compared to a summer's day. Shakespeare. Hennie sifted through the remnants of her university education for a line from the Bard that precisely diagnosed her current state. If she could eloquently describe that sense of dislocation, perhaps it would bring her one step closer to finding some better place. She thought of Hamlet brooding over poor Yorick's skull, a bear pursuing Antigonus, Petruchio stopping Kate's mouth with a kiss. Some of the other girls, she remembered, had been put off by the ending of The Taming of the Shrew (by the entire play, really)—but early on, Hennie had decided Kate's marriage represented the best possible outcome for her.

"Hennie?"

Even before she turned, Hennie recognized the voice. It was the actor from earlier in the day—the tree man, now degarbed, and apparently the man was a woman, a woman Hennie had once known. The tree man was apparently Carly Fenstermacher, and Carly was smiling at Hennie and touching her lightly on the shoulder in the most familiar way, as if they'd had drinks or gone shopping together just last week.

"I'm sorry I chased you off," Carly said. "It was only afterward that I realized those kids must have been with you. I'm so obtuse."

Hennie shifted to let Carly into the booth. Under the table, their knees bumped. Carly adjusted her legs to allow Hennie her space.

"Were those really your children?" asked Carly. "Yowza. That'll make you feel old."

Hennie didn't correct her about Parker, nor did she contradict Carly about the feeling old, even though until that moment she'd always believed the act of raising children kept one youthful. Children—with the way they grew and changed in myriad dimensions, their reaching of milestones and the playing out of their everyday dramas, a pace that only seemed to quicken with each passing year. Children, Hennie believed, kept life lively.

She supposed, however, that Carly had a point, too. You certainly couldn't argue with Carly's appearance—her girlish (almost elfin) figure, everything still high and tight and smooth.

"It's good to see you." Hennie said. She couldn't formulate anything more articulate. "I'm sorry I didn't recognize you earlier. The costume really was very elaborate."

"Thank you." Carly put her elbows on the table and let her face rest on her hands. Her arms were still tinged green from the body paint.

"Where are your little dudes now?" Carly asked.

Hennie had never thought of Corey as a little dude. She feigned nonchalance. "Off on their own. Doing whatever it is boys their age do."

Carly shrugged, letting her shoulders frame her face. Hennie ached with the loveliness of that face, all eyes and lashes and mouth. She remembered how jealous she'd been of those neat rows of teeth, those bursting lips. How daunted when those lips had been offered to her.

"How is Tyler?" Carly asked.

He's an ass, Hennie wanted to say, which was exactly what Carly had told her fifteen years before, after Hennie had broken things off with Carly. If broken was even the word—when she hadn't done anything more than hold Carly's hand; permit herself to be moved by Carly singing her a heavy metal ballad (after they'd both admitted a secret penchant for Warrant); tell Carly that she longed to run out West, to Sante Fe or Denver, someplace at once intimate and anonymous where no one would judge what she did or didn't do, what she was or wasn't. Expressing that desire out loud had mortified Hennie, and the next day, she turned right around and told Carly she was sorry, she'd misspoken, she'd had an ideal childhood by any objective measure, and she owed it (to whom? at what cost?—she'd never thought to ask) to make that kind of life herself, to assemble her own happy family.

Hennie now said, "Tyler's fine." She trotted out the standard spiel, his recent promotion, the write-ups in the local paper, the new venture he was planning. She talked about how well Corey was doing in school, mentioning the robotics camp he would be attending that summer. (While omitting her concerns: that it was his first time away from home; that he was an inordinately picky eater; that although he didn't seek trouble per se, she suspected the wrong peer could pressure him into almost anything.) Carly kept nodding and smiling, but Hennie could almost hear her asking, in that offhand tone that ran directly to Hennie's core: And you're satisfied with this? This brings you joy?

Despite which, Hennie was blathering on about spearheading a new initiative on the PTA Green Committee.

"Well," Carly said, finally. "I guess I should maybe make like a tree…"

"Don't go." Hennie put her hand out on the table. "Please."

Hennie forced herself still. She let her eyes close, let her breathing quiet. She held the air in her chest. And when at last she felt Carly's soft, cool palm, those slim and supple fingers twining about her own, she exhaled softly.

"I think," she whispered, "a part of me has always held on."

"Oh, ho!" cried the obese man with the turkey leg. "She fancies another lady!" He strode over, his drumstick directed at Hennie. "Thou claimed solitude thy desire, when thou desirest the company of the fairer sex."

"Buzz off, Falstaff," Carly said.

The man turned. Switching from the dramatic register, he said, "Spreading your branches, Carly? Adriana couldn't fill your knothole?"

He looked at Hennie again. "Unordinary company, indeed. Spurning Falstaff for a walking tree! How… unconventional."

His entire face trembled, from the folds of his neck to his chin and his jowls, and there was a furious drop of spit at one corner of his mouth. Carly squeezed Hennie's hand. Hennie was aware of the attention of everyone around her, aware of their questions and mirth, their judgment of the woman in foolish pursuit, leaving behind her perfectly reasonable, even enviable existence.

Carly called for her as Hennie fled the bar. Outside, Hennie snaked her way along the path, through the imposters with too much to say, the tourists seeking another life for a day, the happy families, the families just barely hanging on. Hennie ran the way she'd run as a girl whenever her Sunday school teacher scolded her for some minor transgression, forgetting her offering, a simple lapse in attention. She ran until she reached the Faire gates and thrust herself through the turnstile. She didn't bother to have her hand stamped. She'd meet the boys at the gates. There was no need to reenter that place.

She switched on her phone and tapped her husband's name on the display. She put the phone to her ear and kept walking. The line rang once, twice, three times. He would be glancing at the screen, frowning, and setting the phone back down. Returning to his more important worries. Hennie hung up without leaving a message. She walked out toward the parking lot, the makeshift rows of cars in the field.

After a minute or two, Tyler phoned her back. "You called."

Like an accusation. She didn't answer at first. She was almost at her car. Off to one side, among a group of trees, two teenagers were loitering. She slowed, wary of them—vandals? or thieves? But it was only a pair of young lovers.

"Hennie?"

"I'm here." Hennie tried to ignore the couple. She wouldn't begrudge them their naïve bliss, their sloppy urgency, their time unmarred by the concerns and complications and regrets that soon enough would beset them.

"What do you want?"

"I just needed—" Hennie realized she was watching two boys. Two boys were making out. She was close enough to see them plainly. There, in the shade, Parker was putting his tongue inside her son's mouth.

Tyler said, "What do you want, Hennie? I can't hear you. Speak up."

Corey turned toward Hennie as she lowered her phone. Parker reached for Corey's face, but Corey stopped him. He looked directly at Hennie. There was no shame in his expression, no fear.

Hennie had deserted Corey only once. He was two, an age when his need for her was relentless. That day, she begged for privacy in the powder room, and he'd thrown a tantrum. She sat him down in front of the television, switched on Nickelodeon, and walked straight out of the house. She didn't venture far, merely circled the neighborhood a few times, but all the while she fantasized about escaping that miniature orbit and hurtling on with no further purpose or direction than to simply get away.

When the guilt overtook her and she returned to the house, Corey hadn't moved. He glanced at her and then swiveled back to the television. And when the show finished, he asked, in his darling toddler's lisp, "May I please have some juice, Mommy?" The same way he did every afternoon.

"Fuck it," Tyler said, and he hung up.

Hennie opened her arms and said, "Oh, my sweet, sweet baby."

She could almost feel the weight of her son as she cradled him to her chest and nursed him, the rhythm of his swallow in precise time with the beat of her breath, but already Corey was turning away.

Sisterhood

Susan Kress

The fact is adolescent girls benefit just as much as boys do from daily physical exercise. Report from the London County Council Education Authority, 1962

I was not then or now in love
with sports. I was the one not
picked for teams,

the one who loitered
in the locker room, who baulked
at any tussle with a bat

or ball. But at my school, in gym,
we had to pass one test:
to climb a rope.

I learned the art of gripping
with my feet, while
pulling up hand

over hand. One day –
I was thirteen – I first got
to the top.

The rope was taut
against my body – when I
felt the sudden

joy buzz out in stars through
all my limbs – so sharp
it was,

I almost fell. Flushed
with light (or was it dark?)
I saw

the self-same look on
chubby Janice Fisher's face.
Amazed,

we hung there, side by side
on ropes, silent,

dazzled.

Brotherhood of the Midnight Snack
Ellaraine Lockie

He makes it at midnight
An ensemble of garlic fried in olive oil
leftover rice and two eggs as top hats

An elaboration on the long-ago
bread fried in bacon grease
and dressed in Lawry's Seasoned Salt
A rite he brought home from college
into which he initiated his little sister
during summer breaks

We'd eat in the breakfast nook
Lights out to watch fireflies spark the darkness
Curtains breathing in and out of the open windows
after an oven-baked day
Lilacs balming air that carried outdoor
conversations of mosquitoes and crickets

Inside, words sacred between siblings
What really went on at college
and in the fourth grade
Words that built the bridge that would
transport me out of farm life when most stayed

Now between bites of garlic fried rice
We talk of what really goes on in a marriage
a divorce, children, a job
Lights dim to see the birdbath outside the window
The water smooth, polished by the aged moon
An acorn plinks concrete and stills for the night

Purple lilacs shadow the surrounding peace
and a moth flutters a soft motor on the screen
Not a thing except thunder in the throat of distance
to warn us that this would be our last midnight rite

Heart, River
Lita Kurth

They are Americans in Russia. Still in love. The man wanted to go with the woman to Moscow and St. Petersburg, visit white and gold palaces with brocade ceilings where white stairs ascend to a marble heaven. Now they cruise the beauteous Volga River, view its island spires and wide, slow waters.

The man avoids the hundred stone steps to onion-domed cathedrals the color of candy and Disneyland. The man preserves his heart. He takes his medication, drinks his water. He leaves vodka untasted at dinner, lets heavy cream pass by. One day when the boat moors, they walk up to the town; the man has to sit on a bench. He coughs. This has happened before. The woman knows what to do. It's his lungs. He needs to sit up, needs oxygen. She stays with him. Someone calls an ambulance; it comes, and they lay him on a stretcher, close the doors. She can't go along. Terrible sounds arise from inside the ambulance. They have no oxygen.

Her taxi follows the ambulance through sludgy traffic, a river of mud.

At the hospital, they bring him back: unconscious, heart failed, in a Russian hospital. Thank God for translators. Doctors are good here; a kind nurse holds the woman's hand, says words from the heart. The man's room is on the eighth floor but sometimes the woman takes the stairs, which are clean, not dirty.

She wants to be with the man. Every day by cab, she travels the wide, unmoving river of traffic. She sits beside him and holds his hand on top of the white sheet, tells him everything in her heart. Some power translates. His open eyes dream untranslatable dreams. He is on another river, but with her.

She climbs the steps of every day, tries to find the non-rush-hour time—there is none—learns how to Skype the doctor at home, how to add international minutes, how to cope with expiring visas—stay near the hotel; don't go out—how to find someone to translate insurance and conditions, how to arrange an air ambulance. It seems impossible. The ambulance will have to fly at sea level to protect his heart. He will fly with a doctor and a nurse. It will cost $60,000.

Each day, she walks along the park without him just for half an hour. The trees soothe her heart. Lap, lap, lap goes the river against the bank. It is not frozen yet. Sometimes she drinks water. Sometimes she eats a creamy dessert.

She wants to go with him through the air and hold his hand next to her heart. She wants to go home and talk with him about traveling to Moscow and floating the Volga, but that will not be possible. It was his heart. Her own heart will travel alone through the empty air.

What We Talk On When We Trip at Rock Quarries
Jason Arias

Lucy keeps saying how, "Love is love is love," in this sing-song cadence while nodding her head to the right and left, hitting the word love on the downbeat, in the passenger seat next to me.

"Lucy, you sound like a Sunday schoolmarm that's done lost her marbles." I wonder what a schoolmarm actually is. My lips are numb. Or not numb, but just not there. And I wonder if that's the way mediums' lips feel when they're channeling other peoples' words from beyond the end. "Isn't love just not knowing what words will leave your mouth next, but trusting that they're definitely not yours?" I say.

"No," Lucy says. "It's a Beatles song on repeat, on mushrooms. The song that makes you feel sung to and sung about at the same time. Like somebody reading your diary out loud. It's… Sammy are you touching me?"

"No. I don't think so."

"Why not? I feel like you should be touching me."

I start reaching across the Chevy's console without taking my eyes off the horizon because I can't. My knuckles graze the outside of the shifter's plastic blackness, stiff and shiny.

"It's black and stiff and shiny," I say, narrating my own thoughts.

"Maybe yours is. Mine's a periwinkle," Lucy says. "It's, like, the morning fog partially covering the mountains from that seaside hotel balcony that faces south. It's RJ, you know, never knowing that I'm at the edge of the quarry in your car, with you almost touching me, and him being okay with not dying over there and coming back and never knowing. You know?"

I have to think too long about what Lucy is saying.

Could be minutes, could be hours.

"Is it daytime where RJ is?" She says. I can feel the shift of the air when she shakes her head between her sentence rolls. "Why do we call it The Middle East? What the fuck does that even mean?"

"Let me get my head straight, then I'll take you back home," I say. "I promise."

"No," Lucy says grabbing for my hand at the console between us, placing it on the top of her thigh and patting it like she does Miffy, her family cat, when Miffy wants to be somewhere else but she wants Miffy to be with her.

"Why would you say that you were taking me home?"

"Because we shouldn't be here."

"What's wrong, you scared of the dark, Sammy? Hey, can you feel your face?"

"I think maybe my mind's too old for this hallucinogens shit," I say.

While Lucy wants to expand minds, I just want to get mine right. I squeeze Lucy's thigh lightly to let her know that my hand is Miffy deciding to stay put, but that's it. Nothing more. It's nice to have something solid to hold.

Her black leggings feel like the softest thing I've ever felt. I can't not feel them. I keep forgetting her leggings are attached to her. Keep thinking they're attached to what's keeping me from floating away. The stars over the quarry are expanding and contracting around the chords of The Rolling Stones' song Brown Sugar now playing all around us. Or playing somewhere else and here, too. Playing through time maybe.

"My dad used to play this. They trying for a radio revival?" I say.

"These guys never went out."

"I think you're wrong."

My breath is tight and not tight. There's a feeling at the top of my chest where my neck ends that tastes like tree sap. There's tree sap stuck at my neck-end and trickling down the insides of the bones that make up my ribcage. Those soft stars above and beyond us are rearranging themselves into a constellation that looks like That White Dude, Jesus. That White Dude, Jesus's smile is simultaneously unsettling and kind of funny. He's moving his lips to the Stones' song lyrics of Brown Sugar to me.

"Ouch!" Lucy says. "That's too hard."

She squeezes at the fingers that I forgot were my fingers that I forgot were on her leg. She pats my knuckles smooth like Miffy, bringing memory back into them. Her leggings aren't as soft with her muscles all tight. That's good, probably.

"I'm sorry," I say and try to take my hand back, but she pats it still again.

She doesn't say anything for what could be hours, could be days.

Then she does.

"Do you think RJ will come back with all of his legs?"

I want to stop touching her leg now, but I can't.

Instead I say, "That's fucked up, Lucy."

"Yeah, it is. Do you think he'll have all his fingers left?"

The stars aren't That White Dude, Jesus, anymore. The stars are back to just breathing again before transforming into the next thing. Something horrible.

"Do you think he'll come back missing pieces we never even knew he had?" she says.

"I don't know. Of course, he probably will. He'll be missing pieces and we'll be missing pieces. And we'll take turns hiding and seeking them in different places. Why's everything so tight?"

I hate the tightness.

"Yeah. It's like, claustrophobic isn't it?" Lucy opens the passenger door. "Come on."

She stumbles out the opening and there's all the dinging that open car doors make.

The stars aren't anything anymore, they've disappeared into the bright light that's showing me my one hand on my blue jeans, the other on the empty seat. I hear the car door close, taste the puff of air pushed in, clench and unclench my teeth at my reflection in the rearview. I'm me and not me.

The bright light dims slowly, like after the previews, and before the main attraction, at the theatre on Main Street. Then I'm gone.

There's a thunderclap in the car. My car. Our universe imploding. An IED somewhere. And it's terrifying and funny and only a rap on the window to my right that's making me scared. It's Lucy outside, kind of smiling, then too big smiling, then not smiling. The car door opening. Her smiling again.

It's RJ saying "Take care of her, Sammy. Make sure she's not out at the quarry with some fuck, you know?"

There's the inside bright light again and the bright lights behind Lucy—maybe headlights or star things or nothing. I want to tell Lucy something about the softness all around us and between us and within us, and the hardness coming for all of us, but I keep forgetting. I want to tell her how words aren't even things. How my legs feel like they're not attached to me. How I'm not sure I can get out of the car opening. I'm trying, but I keep getting stuck. And RJ's there grinning or screaming or laughing leg-less-ly somewhere in my dad's song, within the Stones' Brown Sugar breakdown.

Lucy takes her hands off of the car door and the car top, puts her arms out to her sides, and starts turning slowly.

"Man. This is. Fucking. Great. Out here," Lucy says, spinning faster and trying not to fall.

Then she falls and catches herself with her hands.

She stares at the dirt ground too long. Not long enough. Forever.

She says, "It's like being born again or something."

Nothing about that sounds good to me. But I manage to get out of the car anyway. The other headlights in the distance have forgotten us or were never there. I put my palms on the cold dirt in front of her. She's cat pose. I'm cow pose. Nobody says anything. We stay like that until every part of me touching the ground feels all of the ground touching me. And when we open our mouths I wonder if we'll never stop laughing and spinning and mooing and meowing.

Genesis

Susan Cummins Miller

Remember when we climbed that limestone tor
out in Nevada? Craving privacy
and summer-hardened bodies we spread your
chambray work shirt under aging pine trees
to shield our naked skin from needles, twigs
and time-etched talus. Afterwards, your head
soft-pillowed on my thigh, we shared ripe figs,
red apples, water—canteen-warm—and bread.
We stared at skies where falcons flew. You tried
to speak—a croak. I brushed ants from my boot.
"This doesn't mean I'll marry you," you cried,
then shied from me and bit into the fruit.
The silence grew about us, hot and still.
We lobbed half-eaten apples down the hill.

No Tugging Today
William Derge

God knows
I don't pretend to understand
the physics of wind and water,
how one hobbles humpbacked under the other,
or how your casting to the northeast
and my casting to the northwest
end uncannily in our neon-colored floats
occupying such a small circle of space
so as to almost entangle one in the other,
yet never touching,
or, if they do,
it must be by one of us
giving a tug on the line to answer a bob.

But no tugging today.
How easily we've turned our interest to our books.
(There was a reason why we brought the chairs and drinks.)
The poles lie odd angles to their lines,
all accessories to an absent contingency.
There is nothing here to catch
that has not already been caught.

Waipahu

Mel Carlson

A slashing wind rattles in the queen palms outside the Stateside Theatre. Sometimes you can't understand what sweet Claudia is saying up there on the big screen. The wind slams green fronds into the louvered air vents that open on the outside walls. Dust blows across the projector's light beams. The usual afternoon sunglow is lost in a dark glowering of overhead clouds. At other times there might be a rosy tint from an Oahu sunset, but not today. Dark gloom pours from the louvers even when lovable Claudia is on screen.

Private Cletus Benton knows Claudia's words by heart. He has been on town duty in Wipe-a-poo, which is what the men call the town, for unhappy hours. He lives in the movie theatre when not on duty. He has seen the movie four times, and he has left weeping with joy each time. He loves Claudia and Dorothy McGuire, who plays her, with an equally pure passion.

The men of Captain Harrison's S2 Section do not believe in purity. "Bullshit." They say. But they cannot tarnish her pure gleam in his shining eyes.

While the wind blows through the louvers, moaning across a taut wire stretched in its path, Cletus sees himself on the sofa before the fire, sitting beside Claudia. He touches her shoulder gently. She presses her cheek against his hand. She unbuttons her blouse. She puts his hand inside her bra on her bare breast. He twists in his theatre seat in contorted agony. Pure girls don't act like that, and good men don't take advantage of them anyway, and Cletus doesn't know what to do next in any case. He doesn't even know what it feels like.

He has driven the men of the S2 section to the brink of bloody violence asking, "What does it feel like?"

"What does what feel like?"

He points to his own chest.

"You mean what does a tit feel like? You stupid son of a bitch." And then they walk away.

The married men bear the heaviest questioning. He follows them around until they become so outraged, they threaten to hit him. Once he was knocked down.

He doesn't care to know about what it feels like in a good time house down on River Street or in the back seat of a car or getting sandy crotch on a dark beach. He wants the pure stuff. Wedding beds.

"How did you do it on your wedding night?" "What do they do they feel on their wedding night, I mean down there?" He rolls his eyes in a wild uncontrolled way. "How does it feel between their legs?" It is always their or them or they as though he were asking for a report on an opposing football team. "Can you look?"

"What?"

"Between their legs. Can you look at it?" This is when the violence begins.

Cletus is a deprived youth. Most soldiers, as boys, played doctor or a similar game with curious girls. Most are at least halfway educated in the ways of men and women, before entering the service. Alas, poor Cletus, a dry bone where the juice of life should be.

There are four customers in the State Side Theatre. A pair of drunken sailors who can't find their way back to Pearl and are too drunk to care, snore in front row seats. Cletus sits precisely in the middle of the middle. The middle is his post in life, except when he screws up, which happens too often.

The Dragon Lady sits in the back row, staring at the back of Cletus's head. She has been watching him all afternoon and into this last evening performance, like a spider watching a ripening fly. She reads his writhing.

She sits down beside Cletus and without speaking and without pause, puts her hand on his inner thigh and strokes it. She is an Oriental lady with the high-arched, plucked eyebrows, scarlet cupid's bow mouth, and white-powder makeup of a Kabuki mask.

"Hand job. One dollah. Blow job two dollah. Three fifty for 'round the world. Money up front. Seventy-five cent rental deposit at my place. No refunds. You want go for broke, gonna take all night and cost full fie dollah." She purses her cupid's bow mouth into sucking motions and makes sucking sounds.

He shrinks from her. He swivels in his seat to see if anyone can see or hear her. He stammers incoherence.

She blows a warm perfumed breath on him. "Hhhhoney hurry up. Sailors waking up. Gotta be this or that, baby. Gotta be them or you. You mo bettah."

He pulls her hand away as if he were removing a swamp leach, stands up and stumbles down the seat row to the exit aisle, where he begins running.

The Dragon Lady rearranges the rear of her very tight shorts and ambles toward the sailors. She is singing snatches of baudy lyrics from the Cockeyed Mayor of Kahalakahoo. The sailors stir. She sits with them.

In the lobby, Cletus smashes into the theatre manager, who is also the projectionist, hurrying to his snack-serving post behind the counter, to empty the oil-reeking popcorn machine for the night.

Cletus backs the manager into the showcase full of Snickers and Hershey bars. He points at the auditorium entrance and shouts. "There is a woman in there putting her hands on people's legs."

"I've never had any complaints." The manager pushes Cletus away. "Let me get behind the counter and I'll mark it down."

"I want her thrown out."

"I'll mark it down."

"Now."

"I'll need witnesses."

"I'll get witnesses." Cletus rushes into the auditorium.

Light from the screen flickers on three contorted figures doing some sort of rhythmical exercises on, across, or in front of the front row of seats. Cletus runs out of the auditorium, past Roy Rogers mounted on a cardboard horse near the front door. Roy grins down at Cletus. You can tell he is about to sing some rollicking cardboard cowboy ditty to Miss Dale Evans or maybe his horse, Trigger.

A block from the theatre Cletus stops at Sushi Joe's Oriental Beanery. He orders egg foo yung, which he heard about once when he was ten. There were no Oriental restaurants in his little Missouri hometown. There were no Orientals. Certainly, there were no Oriental girls in shorts.

He watches the shorts of the two girls paying at the cash register. His hormone levels rise to the top of his head. He has to watch out of the corner of his eye so no one can see the horrible lust that smokes there. Surely God must have invented shorts with the Oriental rear end in mind. The combination is perfection.

Sushi Joe comes to the table. "You okay, soldier?"

Cletus says, "Sure, sure." He stares at the wall behind the cash register while his eyes recover from the shorts. He douses the egg foo yung with an overdose of soy sauce.

"You must be one of the new soldiers in the little house by the sugar mill."

"Yeah."

Joe sticks out his hand. He knows those soldiers are supposed to arrest him and his family in case there is another Japanese attack. Might as well establish friendly relations. They shake hands. The two girls open the front door to leave. Cletus watches their retreating shorts. He thinks "my cup is full and runneth over."

Joe raises an eyebrow. He knows what is happening to Cletus's cup. Cletus knows Joe knows. Blushing he grins at Joe. He asks what time the theatre opens tomorrow.

The Killer Instinct
Marilyn Horn

Carleen had just drained the dish water when she spotted Bud's coffee cup atop the ice box. Time and again she had told her husband to bring his cup to the sink once he was through with it, but there it was, all the way across the room.

She wanted to kill him.

Bud himself was out in the yard, atop a ladder, picking the first ripe apples from the old tree. Whistling. Not a care in the world.

Carleen watched him through the window at the sink. Him and his happy whistling! She twisted the dish towel, wanting to wring his neck.

The silly-sweet voice in Carleen's head always made excuses for him:

At least he didn't leave the cup in the parlor, as he has done before.

Well. His cup would not be washed this morning. No. It would have to wait until tonight.

Maybe he is not done with his cup. Maybe he thought it didn't need washing—

Oh, he was done with it, right enough. He'd drunk up the very last bit of coffee, hadn't he? The coffee pot was bone dry now. Nothing left for Carleen.

He'll make more coffee once he comes in. He often does, you know.

Humph. She smirked and began to dry the cutlery. Maybe he'll trudge through the house in his dirty work boots, too. Tracking in an acre of manure along the way. He often did that, as well.

Surely not an acre!

An acre or more—it felt as much when one swept it out. Oh, Carleen had picked the prize when she married Bud, she surely had.

She wiped the cleaver dry and then ran a finger along the blade. Just a bit more pressure would break the skin.

Yes, a prize. He truly is. Keeping the attic dry and warm for you, whenever a rest is needed…

Carleen scowled at the voice. She had thought about the attic for days now. The attic! It was no heaven on earth.

She put away the cleaver, reluctantly, and stood at the open door. She watched him. He was still atop the ladder and couldn't see her, his back being turned.

He is much too high! He should take care.

Carleen considered. Yes, he was too high. Any old thing might happen. The ladder could tip. A slight nudge with her toe would do it. Who could say it wasn't an accident?

HUSH now. Hush. Please hush.

Carleen wiped her hands on her apron. Over and over she wiped them. She knew just what she would say as she toppled him over, too. "Bud," she would say…

She walked out into the yard.

Stop now. Stop. A rest is what's needed. The attic is quiet and warm…

Carleen got a good ten feet from the ladder and halted. "Bud," she said.

Bud kept on picking and didn't turn. "Steady my ladder for me, will you, dear?"

"Bud," she said again, not coming any closer. Keeping a safe distance between them.

"Yes, my love?" He turned stiffly from his perch and looked at her full on. Carleen noted the change in his expression as he did so; saw the old resigned look overtake him. He climbed down slow and steady and clomped over to her in his muddy boots. "Darling…" He took her hands.

"Bud. Dearest. I think… I think I need my rest."

He peered down into her face but she, ashamed of her wicked thoughts, would not look up. "You think it best?" he asked.

"If you could only hear my thoughts." Her voice caught. For a moment, she could not go on. Then, "If you could hear them, you would know it is best."

A moment passed. "I think you might be right."

So, he had seen the signs these past few days, just as she had.

"The attic is clean," he said. "Warm. All prepared."

Even with the bars on the window, the attic was nicer than the asylum. No ice-cold baths. No restraining ropes. She could still see the sky from the attic. The clouds. The changing colors of the leaves.

"Bud, darling," she said. He had put his arm through hers and was leading her up to the house.

"Yes, dear?"

"It might be best," she said, "the next time around, if you'd bring your dirty cup to the sink."

First Cold

Lisa Masé

Crimson gold maples against
blue sky so fierce
I catch my breath.

The farmer hayed his field yesterday,
leaving round bales behind,
giving the geese no choice but to fly.

Air filled my lungs as they took off
and would not let go until dawn
when the first killing frost
licked each tomato plant,
blackened every marigold,
and finally took my exhale.

Today is bright hope for the soup beans,
greens, butternuts and blue corn that survived,
sweeter now.

You cry in your sleep from your first cold
because you cannot breathe.
My cheek pressed to yours,
we watch chickadees
outside the western window.
They know they must gather
sunflower seeds while they can.

I want to dress myself in leaves
to remember this warm air,
your hot ear and tired eyes,
the learning that comes from fever.

Turn Your Feelings into Animals and Talk to Them
R.R. Shepard

She is driving north, out of Cheyenne. She feels her exhaustion as a cement slab behind her eyes, and the pills aren't helping, not today. The night before, she'd slipped out of the student-parent orientation dinner—Robbie was fine, already had friends, always already had friends—with a tall, bespectacled man who had sat on her left through the speeches. His hands felt as though they'd been dusted in chalk, and his sternum poked out in a little nub beneath his white dress shirt, which had stiff buttons that barely fit through their slits. In a back hallway, between classrooms 106 and 215 (what was the organizing principle, Kay wondered), she brushed her fingers over the nub while he rifled through all eight pockets in search of a condom.

"It's just bone," he said.

"Which bone?" she asked.

He shrugged. "I was born with a club foot," he said, as though that explained it.

The linoleum was freshly polished in anticipation of the new semester, and Kay watched something close to her reflection in it while he fucked her, something halfway between image and shadow.

Kay didn't shower after. As she drives, her jeans chafe at her bareness, and she can still smell him on her. She enjoys taking on the odors of strangers, because unlike sex, she gets to decide when it ends, when she will step into the shower and emerge again, fully, and only, herself.

———————

She is on 487, thirty miles from the nearest gas station and fifty from Casper, when she sees the woman and the bull. She has just been thinking about how the spiky yellow grass of the plains remind her of Robbie's childhood scalp, post-crew cut, and that if you look hard enough it's easy to see the human everywhere in landscapes, and if that's true maybe the opposite is true as well, and that she definitely hasn't had enough sleep, and that starting the moment she gets home she is going to be the person she's been wanting to become, someone who drinks tea instead of coffee, who bathes and stretches before bed, and who takes up some kind of hobby that can't be applied to anything but itself, like curling, or that Japanese flower arranging thing. Robbie and his father might not be directly impressed with this at first, as they will always drink coffee and never arrange flowers, Japanese-style or otherwise. That's fine for them because they don't have the same problem Kay has, of needing to fight to feel even halfway okay like she'll die if she doesn't, like it's really a matter of life and death just to move from A to B and to look human doing it. But she'll get happy, happier even than them, and they'll sure as shit notice that, they'll probably even get jealous, since happiness is the only thing it ever really makes sense to be jealous of.

Kay laughs just thinking about it, the cigarette poised over the gearshift almost all ash, like an old, gray worm, Nickleback on the radio, and all four windows rolled down, when she sees the woman screaming and waving at her, and she sees the bull behind the woman, advancing on her, corralling her against the fence, and Kay careens off onto the shoulder and hurdles out to the trunk, where she finds a lacrosse stick from Robbie's middle school days, a fire extinguisher, and a dirty sock. She takes the first two and runs down the embankment. Her mind is a tendon, serene and cocked. She can hear locusts, or are they grasshoppers? What is the difference? Why don't we ever learn things like that, she wonders. The bull has rammed the woman in the stomach, and she is on the ground coughing and gasping and crying the way kids cry when their parents refuse to notice. Kay swings the lacrosse stick and hits the bull just above the pin bone, but it barely notices, and she can't blame it; it's a cheap stick, plastic, not even aluminum, which Robbie's father purchased at a Walmart in Nebraska.

There are many things that Kay does not know, but she does know the difference between water-based fire extinguishers, and dry ones. Hers is dry, carbon-based, with compressed nitrogen as the propellant. The long, plastic cone will allow the C02 to exit quickly and turbulently from the threaded nipple, expanding and cooling into a mixture of frozen snow and gas, and it will suck the oxygen from the air. She finds this idea magical. She unhooks the safety, aims, and shoots as though it's a Remington. The bull snorts, bucks and runs. She stands in the cloud, listening to its retreat, to a plane somewhere far above, to her breath. Her heart feels like a small, warm, round amphibian she coughed up and has lodged at the back of her throat.

The other woman is fine; a bruised rib, some trauma associated with bulls, but how often will that be a problem? Especially because, Kay learns as they drive, the woman works as a sales rep for Pfizer and doesn't like outdoor recreation. She is the kind of woman who ended up in Wyoming solely because everyone needs to end up somewhere.

They smoke as they drive, and it calms the woman, but not Kay—Kay's elated, like she won the lottery, like she physically bumped into David Tennant, like she just did the world's biggest line. She notices that the woman's thighs spread to the edges of the passenger seat, while her own stay contained within the margins of at least two inches per side, and this, this feeling right here, she thinks, this is happiness.

Kay leaves the woman at a florid green ranch-style house in Casper, in the hands of a husband who seems, in Kay's opinion, overly concerned about the details surrounding this wife ending up in a field, in the middle of nowhere, with a bull. Kay wants to say, "These things happen," but what's the use of intervening in the marriages of others? On the curb outside their house, the man leans on the roof of the car so that from the driver's seat Kay can only see his torso and chin, and says, "Well shit, lady, you're the hero of the day, I guess."

———————

It's dusk. Kay stops at a Conoco and buys a lukewarm breakfast burrito and a black coffee. She isn't home yet, she tells herself as she drives south on 487, retracing her steps. The sky is bruised and almost too big. She hangs her arm out the window while she drives, and when she draws it back in and smells it, the strange man is gone, replaced instead with the wide, clear scent of Western air.

Seated Couple

L M Harrod
after Egon Schliele

There comes this moment
when the beast with two backs
has five legs and neither face
can tell if the extra
is real or prosthetic.
And he says to her,
this is your leg, it wears
your green stocking,
and she says, no, it is
yours, muscular and hairy,
unlike my smooth
and suppliant one,
and why are you
putting on my shoes.
So they try to feel it back
to its source and he
runs his hand up the thigh
until she begins to moan
and he says, see it is
your leg, and she sighs, no,
for she is running her
hand up his thigh and
he is moaning too,
and there it is,
the other leg, anyone can
see as she sits
behind him, as he
sits behind her, five legs
and the fifth belongs
to neither and both, the leg
that everyone touches
and no one knows.

Small Creatures
Catherine Edmunds

I'm carrying my wife to the church one last time, feeling her slim broken body through her clothes. She's quiet now. Somewhere a dog barks, but she won't hear it. I've arrived late, to darkness.

We first came here for our wedding last spring. A woodpecker was going furiously at a cedar in the graveyard. We could even hear it inside the church, tap-tap-tap-tap-tap—and I said, poor thing, I wish we could help it.

Oh, you and your lame ducks, she said, but this is who I am. I may never have mended a broken wing, but growing up, that was all I wanted to do. I tried to revive the creatures the cat brought in, and the pheasant that flew at my father's truck and bounced off. I held it and it knew I was there. It trembled in my hands, there was just me and the dying bird and the softness of its feathers and its eyes half closed, the lower lid raised, its neck loose and flopping. I cupped its body and Father was going to shout at me I'm sure, but there was something about the way I held it that stopped him. He grunted his approval after.

I've known Jenny since schooldays. I was the quiet one who got on with work, never clever enough to shine, never dull enough to get a thrashing. She was the freshest apple off the tree and the smell of crushed mint. She was so far beyond me nothing would ever come of it. She dated one boy and then another and another—and then there was the accident. The boys lost interest. She let me talk to her and she was so sad, so crushed. I told her about the water rat I'd seen twice and the tawny owls nesting where they had last year. I don't think she listened much, but I knew I was helping because she started taking care of herself again and washing her hair and she let me brush it, long and tawny.

One day I brought an injured shrew to show her, so tiny, so delicate. The cat had brought it in, and it didn't have long to live.

Jenny pushed my hand away, she couldn't bear it, said she was afraid of mice.

I think she was afraid of how I held it and what I did, but still she agreed to marry me when the doctors said they could do no more for her legs.

And oh, she was so beautiful at the wedding, and after, when I carried her over the threshold and she was nestling in my arms and her mother was weeping and everyone else was cheering, but that was the last time anything was right.

I've always wanted to mend a broken wing, but I'm not clever enough. All I can do is hold the small dying creatures and let them know I'm here and I won't let them suffer.

Pressure Point
by Rose M. Smith

There's a knob the size of a swollen quarter
just above his navel. An on-off switch of sorts
he's had nearly since born.
Can't turn it like an 80's radio,
tune him into mood to catch the moment,
this sacred bridge between infancy and middle age.

To love it, you must cup the rough hair of his ass
against a warm spoon lap long out of use,
cross the open plain of his broad belly
with a warm embrace, then lie
at the base of his mythology with a gentle hand.
Stroke love into that soft depression
until his body answers.

Don't know why I tell you this.
You have taken space once treasured;
my fingerprints are still embedded in that scrap of skin.
He feels me there, thigh against thigh, warmed
by the curl of my naked mound, feet beneath his feet.
You will not feel the same, I give you this so you can try.

He was mine a dozen years before you called his name,
pulled him back into your world disguised as friend.
You were that kind of friend a man does not share
with his wife, the kind who looks away from her
in grocery aisles and calls to him for comfort
when your man leaves you to raise your kids alone.

I bore him angel fruit, taught them to ride
rough air with silken wings. Forgave him
his absence for a decade. Now you lie beside him
like you've earned your space. To love it, you must cup

the hair of his ass within a warm lap.
Reach across his tiredness,
stroke love into his soft depression.
You will not feel the same to him.
I tell you this so you can try.

What Love Is
Mary Maddox

"I'm gonna marry you when we grow up."

Even then Dee felt unsettled by Mickey's eyes. They were blue, smudged with an emotion she couldn't name. They demanded yes from her.

"Okay," she said.

Yes was easy at age four, when every day went on forever and growing up was unimaginable. Their fathers worked as dispatchers at the railroad station in Soldiers Summit, Utah. A few years later, the station would close, and the town would dwindle to a café and gas station on a secondary highway. It was already in ruins. She and Mickey explored the cellars of houses long ago demolished, rows of square cement holes ranked along a hillside fuzzed with sagebrush. They found dangerous things: two-by-fours with rusty nails hammered through them, shards of blue and green glass, barbed wire. And mysteries: a silver box without a lid, a book with its pages rotted away.

Dee would never forget the smell of those abandoned cellars, the open graves of homes. Spring after spring they collected snow-melt that soaked the remains and slowly dried in the summer sun and wind, seasons of decay like growth rings in a tree trunk.

Just outside town was the ruin of a restaurant, a long single-story building caved in at one end. The walls at the other end stood precariously beneath the weight of the sagging roof. Sections of the floor had been pried up, and the moldering breath of the cellar enfolded Dee and Mickey as they wound between the damage to the restaurant's counter. Drilled holes with blackened edges showed where stools had been bolted onto the floor. But behind the counter was solid floor and an interior wall with shelves. This would be their house, Mickey said. On the shelves they arranged the silver box, the rotted book, and the shards of colored glass.

Under the counter was their bedroom. They snuggled there, his breath warm and damp against her neck.

They were forbidden to play in the ruins, but it was easy to sneak away. Dee's mom was usually busy with housework or laundry and chasing after her two-year-old brother. Mickey's mom stayed inside their house, especially after lunch. When Mom asked where they'd been, Dee said the viaduct or the slope by the train station.

"Don't go near the edge," Mom would say, frowning. "Keep off the tracks."

Dee shook her head in a solemn promise.

One day she announced that Mickey wanted to get married when they were grownups.

"There's no way on Earth," Mom said.

She was shocked by her mother's vehemence. "How come? You like Mickey, don't you? You like his mom."

"You're too young to think about marriage, little girl."

The two families lived next door in the one row of houses still standing. At night she heard Mickey's parents bumping into walls and screaming, and the next morning his mother came over to drink coffee and show Mom her bruises. Mom wheedled Dad to talk to Mickey's father.

"It's none of our business," Dad said. "Stay the hell out of it."

When Dee was old enough for kindergarten, their family moved to Price, and she pretty much forgot Mickey and his family. They sent a card every Christmas. Then her parents got divorced and her father ran off to California. Forced to provide for herself and two children, Mom found a job waitressing at a steakhouse. They moved into a tiny apartment without even a sink in the bathroom. They brushed their teeth at the kitchen sink. She shared a bedroom with Mom since she was too old to share the sofa bed with her brother.

Mickey's mother started coming to visit every few months. She was divorced by now too. While the mothers commiserated over their hardships, their children trooped to Vincent Price double-feature matinees and roamed the aisles of Woolworths downtown. Dee dreaded those long Saturdays with Mickey. It wasn't as bad when his older brother and her younger brother came along. With four of them together, nothing personal could happen. But as soon as Mickey's brother was old enough to stay home by himself, he found better things to do than babysit them. Mickey started ditching her brother so they could be alone together. He loved Dee and planned on getting married their senior year.

"That's four years," she said, awed by the panorama of her future—a landscape vast and empty, with nowhere in it for his presence.

"We could do it junior year," he said. "But we need your mom's permission, I think."

She couldn't always dodge his kisses. They were too open and too wet, heavy with his decaying breath. His body smelled deeply wrong, as though it were designed by nature to repel her in particular. Once he gave her Evening in Paris perfume in a blue bottle like the glass they used to find in Soldiers Summit, and she wondered why he didn't keep it for himself since it was him who smelled funny. She couldn't ignore the pheromonal alarm, couldn't stop herself from cringing whenever he touched her.

"Don't you love me?"

"I just don't want to—"

Mickey accepted her refusal, but he said, "You have to kiss me after we get married."

"What if we don't?"

He looked stunned. "You love somebody else."

"No, I don't love anybody."

Mickey seized her by the shoulders and pulled her against his chest, a sink that made her heart pound with the opposite of desire, its shadow. "I'd rather be dead than live without you."

Dee was dating other guys from her high school, but she'd decided that she would never get married. She was smart, especially in science—smart enough to win a scholarship to college, her teachers said—and she wanted to be a biologist, not somebody's wife. Especially not Mickey's wife. Sooner or later he would figure it out.

During their junior year, Mickey's mother found out she had leukemia and six months to live. She hinted about herself and Mom moving in together so she wouldn't be alone at the end. Mom said no to that. "I won't be her nursemaid," she confided to Dee. "And I can't be responsible for those wild boys of hers." She sounded almost afraid of Mickey and his brother.

So, Mickey's mother depended on a boyfriend to look after her. As she grew sicker, the boyfriend emptied her checking account and took off in her Impala with her checkbook and credit card. The bank statements charted his journey to Kentucky, then Florida, then west again to New Mexico, where the police finally caught up with him. Mickey's brother threatened to kill the bastard but enlisted in the army instead. Only Mickey sat at her bedside when she died.

They drove to Salt Lake for her funeral, a perfunctory service in a funeral parlor instead of church. Not many people showed up, nobody Dee recognized except of course Mickey and his brother, who wore his army uniform and stood manfully beside the casket, a receiving line of one. Mickey wasn't shaking hands with anybody. Barricaded behind the casket, bawling with grief, his face blistery red and torrents of snot flooding his lips, he seemed oblivious to their eyes and judgment. But when his smudged eyes met Dee's, he silently pleaded with her to cross the body of his dead mother and rescue him from despair. He had no other reason to live.

She said, "Mickey, I'm sorry," and stepped aside with her younger brother while Mom offered her condolences. She took care not to look at him anymore.

That was it, she thought. Now he knew they would never be married.

A month after the funeral, Mickey came knocking on their door. Dee glanced up from the Star Trek episode she was watching with her younger brother. Neither of them stirred.

Mom hurried from the kitchen, scowling at their laziness, and yanked the door open. "What in the world!" she said. "How'd you get here?"

"I rode the Greyhound."

"Well, how come you didn't let us know you was coming?" She stood in the doorway, wiping her hands on a striped dish towel.

"I didn't want to cause any bother." Mickey craned to see beyond her head. "It's just a mile and a half walk from the depot. Is Dee around?" He wedged a shoulder between Mom and the door jamb and insinuated himself into the living room.

It was too late in the afternoon for Mickey could catch another bus back to Salt Lake. He probably expected to stay overnight, sharing the sofa bed with her brother as they'd always done when he and his mother stayed. On those occasions Dee had been bumped to a sleeping bag and the two mothers had slept together in the bedroom. She felt suddenly afraid of sleeping in the same apartment with Mickey.

"I have to talk to you," he said.

"Okay." She scooted over on the sofa to make room for him.

"Come for a walk with me."

She glanced toward Mom, appealing for help and getting a watchful stare that left everything to her. She was old enough to make her own decisions. "Let's wait till after this show," she said.

"No. Right now."

"I can't hear," her brother snapped. His eyes hadn't left the TV screen and Dee wondered if he would sacrifice Star Trek to protect them from Mickey if things went that far. Then she thought she must be going crazy. Mickey's mother had died, his brother gone back to the army. He was alone in the world. He needed someone to talk to. She could at least give him that.

"Okay let's go," she said, standing.

"Dinner's going to be ready in half an hour," Mom said. "You get back here. And don't walk in the park or down by the tracks."

"She's safe with me," Mickey said.

They strolled past seedy apartments and bungalows with unkempt yards. She imagined all the buildings were holes in the ground like the ruins of Soldiers Summit. They labored uphill toward the park, the brownish flank of a mountain rising in front of them. The Douglas fir and grass of the park bordered the dusty hillside of scrub and rabbit weed, a wilderness where they could disappear. Dee halted at a picnic table near the street.

"Come and sit down."

"Not here," he said. "I want us to be alone."

"We are alone."

"No, we're not." He blinked nervously at a driveway across the street, where a man was hosing off his boat.

Dee sat on a picnic bench. "What do you want to tell me?"

He knelt on the opposite bench and leaned partway over the table. His eyes had lost their childhood smudge. All their passion had precipitated out of the blue, bent on her. "Why won't you love me?"

"I don't know," she said. "I can't."

"Did you ever love me? Back when you promised to marry me."

She remembered their afternoons scavenging the ruined cellars, his breath stirring against her neck as they snuggled beneath the counter in the caving restaurant, so close to him it was like being with herself. Was that love? "Mickey, we were four years old."

"So, what's changed?"

She couldn't explain how he began to smell wrong, how her skin crawled when he touched her. "We grew up," she said. "I want to live my own life."

"Why can't you live it with me?"

"It wouldn't be mine then."

The planks of the picnic table were painted glossy green. Complicated swirls of dirt left a record of how the rain had dried. A small revolver lay on one plank, both of Mickey's hands cupped around its butt. When had he taken the gun out? Its barrel looked shiny and harmless. Maybe only a cap pistol. Air whispered against her face, which felt suddenly stretched and hot like the skin of a beaten drum. Dee wondered if she should acknowledge the gun.

"What you gonna do with your own life, Dee?" His sarcasm descended fiercely on the word own, the heart of all her cruelty.

"I want to be a biologist."

"Be the mother of my children," he said. "That's biology."

She had nothing to say to that.

Mickey shook his head. "My life is over. Everyone I love is dead or gone away. All I got in the world is you, Dee, and you don't love me. There's something wrong with you. You're incapable of love."

"I'm sorry," she said.

"I'm gonna show you what love is."

He pointed the gun. The mouth of its barrel gaped as if to swallow her whole, and Mickey's inflamed face and chaotic blue eyes took over the world. Her heartbeat thumped inside her skull, bludgeoning every thought as it was born. Caught on the bench, she could neither dive beneath the table nor jump up and run. She waited numbly for the bullet. His mouth stretched in a grimace that she failed to recognize at first. Then something crazy in his eyes—dreamy satisfaction, yawning triumph—gave away that he was smiling. Mickey turned the gun on himself, pointing the barrel under his jaw.

Dee went deaf at the center of the blast. It popped like a bubble. There was blood, a fountain of blood from his splintered face. Her screaming filled the awful cavity. Gore was flashed across the picnic table. She stared down at her arms drenched in Mickey's blood and decorated with tinsels of Mickey's flesh. Then the man who'd been hosing off his boat pulled her clear of the bench and pressed his hand over her eyes.

It wasn't her fault. Everything she came to learn about human emotions and biological drives confirmed her innocence. Every organism on the planet struggles to thrive. She wasn't alive to be his prey, his host, his sustenance. And so, she thrived. She became an environmental biologist and married a man whose skin smelled like maple syrup. They had two sons and a daughter who also thrived. But throughout her life Dee continued to dream of Mickey. Sometimes in the dreams they were children again, scouring the open graves of Soldiers Summit. Clutched in her fist, sometimes, a tiny indigo bottle of Evening in Paris perfume. In scarier dreams she was only aware of his eyes, smudged with passion, watching and waiting for her to betray herself with a word, a gesture, and she felt paralyzed. In the rarest nightmares, the most terrifying, she was drenched in his blood and he was kissing her not with lips but with the blasted hole where his mouth had been, whispering We're married now and now you have to kill me.

Whose voice? Her own or his?

She awoke in a wild panic, clawing at the bed sheets as her lungs clutched for air. Her husband, startled awake, drew her into his arms and murmured the reassurances she already knew. It was just a bad dream. A limbic disturbance, a confluence of chemicals in brain receptors. Nothing more, this stark and indelible claim.

Knocking Off Corners

Charlie Watts

I struggle with things unbroken
because I cannot hold them in the right way.
The round kiss of a child,
a day without expectations,
the beginning, middle and end.

Ridiculous beauty
floods the breath right out of me.
Snow in the cedar outside our window and
        the curve of you pressed up against my stomach,
darkness like a big next chapter racing over us.

Our plan was to grow up together
Knocking off the corners till we fit just right.
I had trouble understanding
        that it is better to hold your own soul
than to ask someone else to do all the care and feeding.

So I'm asking you to teach me
the warm necessity of things unbroken.
The unpressured holding of hands,
the cat's stretched-out paw, resting on the head of the dog,
hot coffee with cream, and sugar.

Love

D. Dina Friedman

Roberto was frying eggs. Shanti was considering going vegan, even though she knew the chickens personally. They were from the free-range farmer down the road who had a reputation for golden yolks.

"These are wicked stuck. You need a Teflon pan," Roberto shouted over the television. Shanti dug her new manicure—metallic blue—into a bowl of popcorn and continued to watch the news. Always bad these days.

"It's a wicked mess!" Roberto repeated the New England slang he'd recently appropriated, so weird sounding with his accent. "My Mami would hate this wasted food."

Shanti didn't need to pay attention. She was unlikely to ever meet his mother, who lived in Guatemala. Her mother, a Marin County art gallery owner, had raised her on high-quality cookware. "I'm a cast iron girl." She yawned to emphasize how bored she was by his obsession with crumbs.

Roberto sliced their sunny-side-up dinner into two equally sized pieces and poured the rest of the cabernet they'd started the night before. They ate quietly, stealing glances at the CNN headlines: immigration crackdowns everywhere, the latest accusations of voter fraud. After dinner, Shanti washed the dishes and played an imaginary conversation in her head with that hot Chinese guy who kept coming into the library to take out film noir DVDs, her mind quickly fast-forwarding to moving in with him, bonding over vegan stir-fries in a cast iron wok. The fantasy was ridiculous, but she couldn't help herself. She wished someone would give her a love potion—something that could entice her to trust in the overall goodness of things she already had.

Shanti had met Roberto at a bar in New York last November, the weekend after Brett had broken up with her. "You need a wild-girl mission," her best friend Mallory insisted. "Come visit, and we'll find someone to take your mind off that asshole." Shanti had been so drunk, she hadn't remembered much of their first night together, other than the gentle way Roberto had taken her arm when she felt herself tilting on the subway steps, and how he asked if she was sure she wanted to be with him before they started kissing and whatnot. "If you don't, it's okay." He leaned in as if her answer would actually be important, and she was touched because no one at all those frat parties had ever asked her what she wanted.

He lived in a small room on the top floor of a rowhouse, in a neighborhood with loud Latin music blaring in the streets and the subway rumbling above them. In the morning, when she opened her eyes to the piercing light from the bare bulb on the ceiling that zinged like a laser to her throbbing head, Roberto brought her an aspirin and toast. After she ate, they walked through the dirty streets of Queens, past stores barred closed with iron gates. "I need to tell you something," Roberto took her hand and ran his tickly palm back and forth over her knuckles. The gesture felt so intimate, much more than what she could remember of the sex from the night before. "I'm illegal."

No human being can be illegal. Her parents' rhetoric rang in her head. They'd done a show on the art of undocumented immigrants.

As she was about to say those words out loud to let him know she was cool, Roberto told her about the soldiers taking his father away when he was seven years old, and how he hid behind a haystack for hours until his Mami came to him crying. "You must be my little man, now," she said.

They never saw Papi again. They moved to the city where every day after school he'd sit in the square and do bird whistles or play plastic flutes, anything to inspire the American tourists to throw a few coins in their direction. "They looked so rich. Not just their clothes, but their faces. They were so smooth without worry lines—it seemed unreal," he said. "Like magic. That's how I thought of this country. Like a magic place."

She and Roberto stopped at a bodega and drank lukewarm coffee that tasted like old pots. Roberto's accent thickened, his words rushing into each other as he continued his story—a day shortly after his sixteenth birthday, when he left Mami at his uncle's farm and headed north, taking odd jobs as he made his way through Mexico until he'd saved enough to pay the coyote to take him across the border. He immediately hitched to New York, a place he thought would be easiest to slip under the radar. He'd been lucky, he told her, and he was grateful to El Señor for the community he'd found—Jorgé, especially, who let him work in his garage and taught him everything he knew. But now with the recent election, the bad feelings about immigrants so thick in the air, he was scared.

"So, move in with me. I live near Canada. We can sneak you over the border."

It was a wild-girl thing to say. Roberto reached over to kiss her, as hard and long as if she might be saying, "I do." and Shanti couldn't help but project herself into a fantasy wedding scene, even though she knew the idea was motivated by practicality, not love. But hey, he needed help, and Brett had told her she was too shallow and apolitical. "You have no values," Brett had flung the words at her after he found out she hadn't bothered to vote. Shanti knew this was just an excuse, since he was already sneaking around with Carly. She should have stayed in Burlington when Brett got into law school, rather than accepting the job at the historic library that spanned the U.S./Canadian border. But she'd worked at the library in college and thought she might want to be a librarian. And now, she realized she'd accepted that job for a higher purpose: providing Roberto a Canadian shelf to hide behind if la migra ever bothered to come to a remote little hamlet like Derby Line, Vermont.

When she went home after the weekend, Shanti felt much better, though not better enough to stop sending text rants at Brett, or fantasizing about the hot Chinese guy, who had just started coming into the library. Still, it had been nice to feel loved, even if just for a weekend. She didn't think Roberto would really move in, or that she'd even see him again, but he started calling and they'd spend hours in flirty sex talk on the phone. Then they rendezvoused at Mallory's apartment to take care of her cat over Christmas, and shortly after the inauguration, Roberto did come to live with her, this time not asking if it was what she really wanted.

Roberto found work with no problem since Vermonters make a point of holding onto their pick-ups for as long as there's enough metal to bridge the rust. He sent most of his money home to his mother, except for what he gave Shanti to help with the food and rent, and the times he'd gotten her a surprise, like the quilt he'd found at a local craft fair, a fusion of solid New England crafting and bright Guatemala colors. Even though the sex was good, Shanti wasn't too sure about their future. They had too many stupid disagreements about things like Teflon. And, she had to admit, she was still hurting from her breakup with Brett, and she couldn't stop thinking about the Chinese guy, though all she'd managed to say to him so far was to ask if he wanted a written card with the due date or an email reminder. She hadn't even remembered to look at his library card long enough to learn his name.

As the last rays of sun sank behind the mountain, Shanti shut the window and got the quilt Roberto had bought off the bed, wrapping it around her bare shoulders and tucking the edges under her toes, as she sat on the couch and tried to read Noam Chomsky (Brett's book recommendation). Even in June, the nights in northern Vermont were ridiculously frigid.

"*Querrida*." Roberto lifted a corner and turned her chin. She opened her mouth and they kissed. She did love his Spanish sweet talk, and the sturdiness of his body when he held her.

"*Mi corazon*." Roberto squeezed her close. She mashed her face into his. As their clothes flew over the rim of the couch, Shanti closed her eyes and tried not to think about the Chinese guy. She ran her hand along Roberto's smooth chest and breathed in his scent—always that slight residue of auto grease tinged today with the pleasant, homey smell of eggs and onions.

She was falling into that place where nothing mattered except the anticipation of a dramatic and splendorous crash, when the doorbell rang. Who would be here now? She ignored it.

"Police!"

Why would the police be here? A fire? A break-in?

She untangled herself and threw on the sundress she'd just taken off, then opened the door and found herself looking straight into the cold eyes of two ICE agents.

"Roberto Garcia."

He was still lying on the couch, stunned from the sudden switch from romance to horror flick, the quilt his only barrier between la migra and his all-togetherness. As they grabbed Roberto and cuffed his hands behind his back, Shanti was struck by the starkness of his naked skin against the man's uniform, how vulnerable he looked against the man's black shirt with the big white words, "POLICE" and "ICE." They ignored his request to put on his clothes, though they draped what looked like a green and itchy woolen blanket around him and let Shanti gather his things and put them in a bag. "You'll get a jumpsuit at the detention center," one of them chuckled.

"Where?" Shanti screamed. "Where are you taking him?" But they simply grunted and led Roberto through the door and into the cruiser.

Hysterical, Shanti called Mallory, who helped her search the web for an immigration hotline. The woman who answered sounded bored, but she said they'd try to track Roberto, as if he were a dog or something on radar, or as if they could pick up that slight car-greasy scent. The woman took Shanti's number and said she'd call back, but Shanti didn't believe they would really do anything. She paced the living room, wondering who else she could call. Her mother? His mother in Guatemala? Other than Mallory, she hadn't told anyone about Roberto's status. How was she going to find him? She was so stupid! Why had she opened the door? Brett's harsh words rang in her ears. *The world's falling to pieces and all you do is read fantasy novels. You don't even vote!*

She grabbed a jacket and got in her car.

The whole way to Burlington, she insisted to herself that she wasn't engaging in magical thinking. Brett knew people. He understood better than she did how these things worked, and he had a sharp fighter's edge. It wouldn't have to be personal. But she couldn't stop herself from writing reconciliation scenes as she got off the highway and began the long trek down the twisty road that separated the eastern part of the state from the west, contemplating the best option for the perfect outcome. Would it be better to text first—tell him she needed his advice? Or just show up, hoping he'd be jealous when she told him the problem was about another man. "A lover." She'd linger on the word as long as possible.

Shame on her. Roberto was in trouble. He had to be her focus.

She sent Brett a quick text saying that she had an emergency and was coming over to get his help. Certainly, that would be enough of a warning to get Carly to disappear. Their old apartment in a run-down clapboard house looked alien to her when she pulled into the driveway. The door had been painted bright red, and the porch seemed even more tired. The old sofa that they'd found on the street and would sit on for hours watching the world go by had a gash in the seat. Bits of stuffing spilled out of the crack.

She rang the bell and Brett opened the door, wearing a Red Sox cap and UVM sweats. "What?" His voice was terse. "I've got a big exam tomorrow and I have to study."

"I need your help. My boyfriend…" she waited for a reaction—a sucking in of breath, or twist in his facial expression—but there was none. "My lover… ICE just came and took him away. He's an undocumented immigrant. I don't know where he is!"

"And I'm supposed to know?"

"I thought you'd know how to find him."

"I'm not an immigration advocate. I'm just a law student, for Christ sake."

"I thought you cared about these things. You broke up with me because you said I didn't care, but I do. You're a hypocrite!" she was screaming at him now, loud enough that the neighbors might hear, but she didn't care.

"Shanti, calm down." That voice again, terse and dismissive. He was going to be one of those shark lawyers people made jokes about. Why had she ever liked him? Or thought she loved him?

"All right," he said. "We can get you some contacts."

Shanti didn't like the word "we." Carly must be here.

"I already called someone. They said they'd try to track him, but I don't think they knew anything."

"I can find you good resources." Still blocking the threshold, he pulled his phone out of his pocket. "Here's a website where you can locate him." He handed her the phone.

Shanti searched for Roberto's name. "New Hampshire," she said. "Dover. How far is that?"

"I don't know. Ask the GPS. Just get a good night's sleep and call in the morning. I know a couple of places that work on immigration. I'll text you the numbers."

"Can I stay here?" Her voice was small. "I won't bother you—and Carly—I promise. I'll sleep on the couch. I just think it would be better, since I came all the way to Burlington, if I could talk to a lawyer in person."

Brett scowled. "Carly's visiting her parents in Boston. You can stay on the couch, but no love talk. No talk at all. I've got to study."

He made up the couch for her, flinging the sheets so hard they snapped as they unfurled. "I don't have extra blankets," he said. And while she thought the gentlemanly thing to do would be for him to give her a blanket from his bed (or, perhaps invite her to sleep with him—as friends, of course, no touching) she simply nodded and thought of Roberto, naked under that itchy blanket, who had spent so many nights sleeping on the streets of Guatemala, or in the deserts of Mexico.

"I have class at eight tomorrow," Brett said. "So, you'll have to get up early and be out by seven." He turned away from her and walked into the bedroom, clicking the door.

Shanti went out to the porch and called her mother in California.

"Don't get too involved," her mother said. "They might send you to jail."

"But…"

"I know, honey. I'm just worried about you. You shouldn't have let him move in. Make sure to talk to a lawyer before you do anything."

A group of noisy summer students came down the street on their way to the bars. Shanti remembered her first summer in Burlington, how magical it seemed then, so easy to get a fake ID and drink all you wanted. She wouldn't mind going out and getting totally drunk right now. Maybe she'd meet someone and wouldn't have to stay here tonight. But she wasn't heartless enough to betray Roberto, and she needed to be at the top of her game tomorrow. She couldn't risk waking up with a hangover.

Not that she slept much that night. She was cold, the couch was lumpy, and she couldn't stop thinking about Roberto—and about Brett and how rude he was when all she wanted was a little comforting.

"You really don't care," she confronted him in the kitchen the next morning while he made his breakfast as if she weren't even there, not even offering her a cup of coffee or a bowl of cereal. "You think you're so woke, but you're an asshole!"

"Not now, Shanti. I've got a big exam."

"And I have a boyfriend who was just taken to a detention center!" She stormed out, slamming the door and revving the motor. At least the melodramatic exit was better than her tears the last time she'd seen him. She was glad to be out of there.

At a café downtown, she texted her boss and told him she was sick. Then she called the detention center in New Hampshire. No visiting hours until tomorrow. They'd give her message to Roberto, but no guarantees he'd be able to phone her back. After that, she called the number Brett had given her. They told her to come right over, and she was finally able to cry in the arms of an immigration counselor, who told her the next step was to get Roberto a lawyer and raise bail money so he could be released until his hearing.

If she got him out, maybe he could sneak through the back window of the library into Canada, Shanti thought, temporarily ignoring the fact of the surveillance cameras that she knew surrounded the oddly situated building. Should she go with him? She thought about her mother's warnings and asked the counselor if she was also in trouble. The girl told her she'd done nothing illegal as long as Roberto hadn't already been ordered to be deported, but if he had deliberately violated a deportation order, she could be arrested for harboring him. "Usually, we try to get a church involved in those cases," she explained. "ICE generally won't go into a church—at least, most of the time."

They found her a lawyer, a stocky older woman named Miriam Katz, who told Shanti her life story as they drove to the detention center in New Hampshire, braving the bumps in Miriam's old Subaru Outback, which clearly needed work on the shock absorbers. Miriam told Shanti she'd been a lawyer in Brooklyn with a summer place in Vermont, where she'd come out of retirement to help "fight these bastards." Miriam drove like a New Yorker, honking at any car that was going slower than she wanted to go, and pulling out to pass at the narrowest of opportunities. "You should have never let the police in," she scolded. "They're not allowed to enter a home without a warrant. Did you see a warrant?"

When Shanti started to cry again, Miriam patted her hand. "It's not your fault. It just shows we're not getting information to people who need it. And maybe I can argue that he was arrested illegally, but in any case, we should be able to get him out until his hearing. They might post a large bail. Do you have resources?"

Shanti wondered whether her parents might lend her bail money. They were liberals, after all. But her mother had been so hostile, worrying only that she might be breaking the law. Who else had money? Mallory was barely making it, juggling acting classes and trying to pay New York rents on her hostess job. Brett came from a rich family, but she had to stop the fantasy thinking. She was through with Brett.

Miriam told Shanti to wait in the lobby. "I'll try to get you in to see him. "But the more important thing right now is to get him out of jail." She disappeared behind the closed doors.

The waiting room had orange vinyl furniture and an ugly black clock with white numbers that made noise each time the second hand ticked. Her phone was already on half battery and she had forgotten her charger, so she turned it off and thumbed through People magazines for an hour, then another.

"Okay, two thousand," Miriam said, when she finally reappeared. "They should never have taken him. He has no record, at all. These bastards…"

"Two thousand? That's insane!" Shanti only had around five hundred dollars in her savings account. Her salary was low, her loans were high, and she'd always been the type to be seduced by items of the moment.

"It's actually extremely low. They're jacking up bail like crazy. Maybe there's someone you can borrow money from," Miriam said. "I can't help you. It would be an ethics violation. I got to speak with him, though—he's a lovely man. You've done well! He told me to send you his love."

"They won't let me see him?"

Miriam shook her head. "I said we drove over three hours to get here, but they don't care. They said you had to come back during visiting hours tomorrow. I guess you could find a place to stay and go back on your own. I can take you to a hotel or rent-a-car place, but I have to be in Burlington for a board meeting at six."

"No, I'll go with you. I have to try to get bail money together."

"Okay. As soon as you have the money, I think we can get him out."

Miriam was quieter on the way back, listening first to classical music and then muttering soft curses at the news items on NPR while Shanti debated the pros and cons of contacting Brett. He'd been generous when they were dating, always buying her expensive presents and taking her out to dinner at fancy restaurants. Two thousand dollars would be a blink to him—and she'd pay him back.

She sent a text as they crossed the Vermont border, keeping her tone light as if the fight they'd had this morning never happened. Thanks so much for the referral. I have an awesome lawyer, but I need bail money. Any chance you can lend me?

Every five minutes she checked her phone for an answer. His exam certainly would be over by now. Maybe his phone was dead.

Finally, he pinged back, just as they crossed into Burlington. I think it would be better for both of us if you used other resources.

Shanti was still tempted to stop at his house and ask him in person, but she talked herself out of it, deliberately making an out-of-the-way turn so she wouldn't have to drive past his street. As she got off the highway and began to climb the mountain road toward home, she felt lighter, even though it had started to thunderstorm and she had to put the wipers on high and drive super slowly to see the curves in the road. Maybe her boss could give her an advance on her salary, or she could sell some stuff, the pearl necklace Brett had given her for her last birthday, packaged in that little square box she had thought was going to be an engagement ring. That had to be worth a few hundred.

After work the next day, she packed up everything in the house that could possibly be valuable and drove to the pawn shop a few towns away. She came back with a thousand dollars. With her five hundred in savings, she only had five hundred more to go. Her boss told her it was against regulations to get an advance, but he personally lent her two hundred and fifty. She found a few more pieces of jewelry. Then she went into the bedroom and saw the quilt. It made the bed look so naked when she folded it up, but there was nothing else that could be done.

She called Miriam Katz and arranged to wire the money. The next day, Roberto called from New Hampshire and told her he was free. She said she'd pick him up as soon as she got off work.

As she was getting ready to close the library, the Chinese guy came in to return Casablanca. His khaki shorts hung low on his hips and he was wearing a sea-green collared shirt that was open halfway down his chest, revealing a gold chain that sparkled, even under the library's dull fluorescent lights. Despite herself, Shanti felt her heart beating harder.

"Great movie." She gave him the smile she had practiced.

"Yeah, I think I've seen it like a hundred times. ... that scene on the runway. I could watch it forever." He smiled back, meeting her eyes in a brief lock. "What's your favorite classic?"

"Not sure," she said, as Thelma and Louise, proclaimed endless times by her mother as the best move ever, suddenly popped into her head. "Casablanca's definitely up there."

"Do you like Hitchcock?"

"I do." She gazed at the ends of his shiny black hair, which curled under his ears and hoped he wouldn't ask her to prove it. The only Hitchcock movie she remembered seeing was Psycho, and that was at a midnight college film event when she and Brett were newly dating and too busy making out to pay much attention. "Scary stuff ... but it's so awesome."

"They're doing a Hitchcock festival across the border in Magog next week." He pushed a copy of You Only Live Once, along with his card, across the desk. His hands were long and slim, and he was close enough that she could smell a slight odor of mint on his breath. "Maybe you'd like to come with me."

Shanti took the card and glanced at his name—Sean Chen. He was gorgeous. She felt a pang of excitement, a shortness of breath as she imagined closing her eyes and burying her head against his beautiful chest in a dark old movie theater.

But it was not to be.

"Thanks." She stared at the computer as she scanned the item. "I'm in a relationship."

"Oh." He looked embarrassed as he took the card and the DVD out of her hand. "Sorry. Thought you were flirting."

She watched his perfect butt wistfully as he hurried out the door.

————————

Shanti found an oldies station with a strong signal that took her all the way to New Hampshire and sang along with Blondie and Madonna. Roberto was waiting in the lobby with the ugly clock when she got there. His face looked older and more craggy, but she saw the lines in it lighten as he bounced up and took her in his arms for a long, movie-star kiss. "I knew it was a gift to find you," he said. "A gift from *el Señor*."

On the way home, Shanti kept the oldies station on low while Roberto slept. He'd had little sleep since his arrest he told her, though he wouldn't say too much else about his treatment at the jail, no matter how much she asked him. "I'm fine," he said. "That's all that matters, *gracias al Señor*. The lady, Miriam, she said they'd tell me when is my hearing. It won't be for a few months. I can figure out what to do."

As usual, the night was cold when they arrived home, the temperature well below fifty. Shanti thought about turning on the heat, but she didn't want to run up the bill, now that she owed so much money.

"We'll just have to keep each other warm," she let her voice go light and flirtatious as she led him into the bedroom.

He stopped when he saw the quilt-less bed. "What happened?"

"I had to pawn it to raise your bail money. Along with some jewelry and stuff."

"No, *querrida*, that was for you!" He reached for his wallet and shook out three twenties and a ten. "We'll go to the pawn shop and get it back. If this money isn't enough, I'll work overtime."

"It's okay for now." She found an old moth-eaten blanket at the bottom of the closet and put it on the bed. "Like I said, you can keep me warm."

That night, she held onto his body as if they really were long-lost lovers with a connection as intense as Bogie and Bergman—a spicy and resonant love scene she'd keep rewinding in the bittersweet months that followed, their continued arguments about cookware, the hearing, the appeal, and the final order to buy a plane ticket to Guatemala.

She kissed him goodbye at the airport, inhaling her last whiff of his fried-egg and car-grease tinged skin. When they pulled apart, he reached out gently to steady her in front of the TSA check, where she thought she might collapse from the grief of it all. She wanted to say something memorable and classic like, "We'll always have Vermont," but she knew he wouldn't even get the reference. And she wouldn't be able to stand on the tarmac watching the plane take off with that look of nearly fatal hurt emanating through Bogie's resolute and crusty exterior.

So, she simply closed her eyes and kissed Roberto one more time, a gentle peck not even worthy of fade-to-black, a moment fated to unravel that couldn't be tempered by her fantasies, no matter how much she tried to hold onto them. Then she went home to bury herself in the quilt, which would forever smell like eggs and car grease in her mind, no matter how many times she washed it.

The Ride

Morrow Dowdle

It's a space only she could inhabit,
the slender distance between my body
and the back of the dining room chair.

It's a space only she would think to enter,
this only body who has lived inside me,
climbing into this narrow gap,

so close that she has to wrap
her arms around my belly,
her legs around my hips to fit.

We're sitting on a motorcycle,
faces hopeful in the chrome,
riding out our first time

trying out life as parent and child,
tranquil in this seat
as wind whistles through our hair.

She has no idea what I'm packing
in these saddlebags, no conception yet
of a three-generation hiatus

on love between mothers and daughters
and how hard we're going to fight
to end it.

Company
Neil Brosnan

The racket disrupts her all too brief slumber. The frantic lowing, the spluttering bowel evacuations, the slithering of cloven hooves on slimy concrete, the lunging of heavy bodies against metal barriers: the unique sensorial amalgam that heralds the most dreaded day of her year—but this year more than ever. She recognises the bellow of each cow, the bawl of each calf, and so she should. Has she not assisted at every calving and lambing since his accident?

Subconsciously, she filters through the cacophony, her ears straining for a hup, cully, or a lie down, Sal, or the hiss of an expletive spat at an overprotective mother. Suddenly wide awake, she spins sideways, and reaching a reedy arm through the gloom, feels for the switch of her bedside lamp. Blinking sleep-encrusted eyes against the sudden glare, she is only mildly surprised that her alarm clock reads twenty minutes shy of seven o'clock. Why hadn't he roused her? Has she not warned him against tackling such tasks alone? What will it take to make him realise that he is not invincible? Is he not the one who is constantly warning about the volatility of today's livestock, that each generation of sucklers is more feral than its predecessor? She swings her feet to the cool of the linoleum floor and sweeping her dressing gown from its hook on the door, pads across the hallway to his room.

Reaching the pale rectangle of window, she probes for the drape edges and jerks them apart. Heart pounding, she slaps her trembling palms on the window ledge, and then lets her breath escape in a long sigh of relief. He is there—upright—his hatted head haloed in the yellowish glow of the yard light, his splayed elbows resting on the top bar of the crush, the back of his waxed jacket towards the house. The dark outline of Sal is by his side—half-sitting, half-poised for action. Mirroring his stillness, she watches for several moments, marvelling at how quickly the steaming cattle respond to his soothing voice. Even Sal now seems more relaxed, the coil of her feathery tail only occasionally twitching against the damp of the yard.

Things could have been so different, she muses, swirling a ripple of oil around the warming frying pan. Life would be so much easier if the sale of the bridge inch had materialised. Despite his innate aversion to parting with any land, she'd had little difficulty convincing him that those two acres had always been more hindrance than help to his daily farming efforts. Initially, he had belittled the idea of anybody building anything on the narrow strip of marshland, but with no less than three developers vying to outdo each other with obscene offers, he'd finally begun to believe their days of scrimping and saving might be coming to an end. With a SALE AGREED sign about to be erected by the bridge, came the implosion of the Celtic Tiger, and if that wasn't bad enough, she had returned from a neighbour's funeral a few weeks later to find him lying in the empty hayshed, his right foot pinned beneath the low loader he had been working on.

The backdoor latch sounds. Reversing inside, he removes his jacket, hat, and wellingtons, and then rinses his hands under the scullery tap. As her eyes stray to the flip-flopping toe of his right sock, she reflects on the incongruity of pain continuing to recur in digits long since amputated. He is quite sanguine about his two lost toes, quipping that he gains a full hour each year by having fewer toenails to clip. He occasionally reminds her how she had passed her driving test at her first attempt following his injury, despite having failed on five previous occasions. She no longer comments when having to replenish depleted stocks of whiskey and paracetamol, neither does she complain when the sounds of TV channel-hopping continue well into the small hours. She cracks a second egg against the rim of the pan, both pleased and jealous at the thought that he'll take several drinks before she'll bring him back home to the dinner she'll have warming over a saucepan on the turf-fired range.

"Thanks," he says, draining his mug and rising from the table as the haulier's truck rattles into the yard "that was great. You'll turn them out in a while, so?"

"I will," she nods, starting to clear the table. "Good luck. Ring me when you're ready."

The loading goes smoothly: haulier, farmer, and dog dovetailing perfectly to cajole the skittish calves from their pen to the clatter of the steel-reinforced aluminium ramp. As the haulier secures the tailgate, the collie's determined efforts to follow her master into the cab of the truck bring a twinkle to her eyes. Once the haulier starts his engine, she abandons her vigil at the kitchen window and hurries to the front door in time to see Sal go through an elaborate sequence of circles and figures-of-eight, while vociferously escorting the truck to the cattle grid between the entrance piers. Pulling the door shut behind her, she clicks the dog to her side, and crossing the yard, opens the gate to the small paddock where mothers and young had spent their final night together. The few calves remaining on the farm graze contentedly in the large paddock at the other side of the gravelled passage, along with the bull and the mothers they will eventually replace. He was right about the grass, she affirms. Short of a deluge, a blizzard, or severe early frost, the stock should need neither foddering nor housing before December.

Approaching the pungent maelstrom of the crush, she winces. The pecking order is being ruthlessly reinforced with headbutts and sideswipes to the unprotected bellies of inferiors. She draws the shooting bolt, and only too familiar with the propensity of an ungrateful beast to make a parting charge at its liberator, clambers aboard the cab of the pre-positioned tractor. She can't resist a smile at Sal's superfluous to-ing and fro-ing at the rear of the pen. The canny collie is just as aware as she that cattle are more easily scattered than gathered. She alights from her perch in time to see Sal make a token swipe at the heels of the hindmost animal, a surly Charolaise from which almost half of the herd is descended. With a disdainful snort, the old cow flicks a hind hoof towards the dog, and then, head tossing, prances into the paddock. The frolicking of the old matriarch triggers the entire herd into an ungainly, plunging ballet. Smiling absently, she secures the gate and then bends to ruffle the damp of Sal's white scruff.

The spectacle is brief. The animals quickly calm and divide into little grazing huddles. She particularly enjoys being privy to such occasions, and never ceases to be in awe of the dynamic within the herd: how proximity of birth dates rather than bloodlines determines to which grouping each individual belongs. It's almost as if these great lumbering creatures have already adjusted to the loss of their young, just as human mothers must accept the inevitable severing of the apron strings. It's an experience she will never have. Perhaps it's just as well, considering the wave of all-consuming jealousy that had engulfed her when he had introduced her to the girl who runs the egg and poultry stall at the town's weekly farmers' market. Recalling her horror at the thought of that creature's people coming to walk their land, she feels her dentures gnaw at her upper lip. No. She may not be his mother but she is old enough to be, and other than nursing him at her breast, she has done as much for him as any mother could. The thought of that little trollop's bare legs stretched beneath her dinner table, or on her couch, not to mention in his bed, had been too much to contemplate. She had told him so, pointing out that the girl's blonde hair was no more real than the diamante stud that sparkled above her left nostril.

He is, after all, her only family, and has been since their father's merciful release from the stranglehold of dementia. She hadn't long turned sixteen when he was born, but she has never been sure whether she'd been told about his birth before or after she'd learnt of their mother's death. Mam had just turned forty—sixteen years younger than she would be on her next birthday. Sixteen features a lot in their lives. She is sixteen years older than her brother, Dad had been sixteen years older than Mam, and Dad had lived for sixteen years after Mam's death. Today is the sixteenth of October and today he has taken sixteen calves to the mart.

The rain has started again. Not proper rain, but that sticky sort of drizzle that creeps up on you and seeps through every stitch of your clothing almost before you're aware of it. Shivering, she realises she hasn't yet fed the hens—or even released them from their coop. The hens are not producing at present. Otherwise, the coop would have been her first port of call. There is nothing like a freshly laid egg to start the day. She scatters a few fistfuls of oats around the lattice-wired run, and then opens the door of the coop. All five of her remaining hens are well past their prime. She knows she needs new stock—half-a-dozen young pullets would be a godsend—but having to smuggle, and then burn, supermarket egg boxes is preferable to dealing with that trollop at the farmers' market. Mam was a great woman for her hens, she'd have a couple of dozen at any given time: factory incubated leghorn/Rhode Island crosses, which she would buy as day-old chicks. To this day she has no idea how the breeders could guarantee the sex of those little creatures. Hens and eggs had been a business to Mam, every bit as much as livestock and milk had been to Dad. If anything, Mam had been the more ruthless when it came to profit margins. Long before yellow tags had appeared on the ears of cattle, every new pullet would be fitted with a coloured plastic leg ring before being assimilated into the flock. Each colour: red, yellow, or green denoted the year of a bird's hatching. Mam hadn't needed more than three colours: to Mam, any hen allowed to live beyond her third year was guaranteed to die in debt. Shuddering involuntarily, she seeks the shelter of the hayshed.

While she has inherited many of Mam's traits, there is a lot of Dad in him, but in a good way. He is better rounded, more open to others' points of view. Although she sometimes sees this as a weakness, she has to admit that their relationship couldn't have endured if he shared her intransigence. He is a very good farmer, always ready to embrace new systems and ideas without dismissing the methods and philosophies of the past. His efficiency is reflected in the quality of the stock, the functionality of the outbuildings and yard, the well-maintained fences and passages, and the productivity of the land. It's no surprise how the farm has thrived under his stewardship. His intelligence had been evident even in childhood. She has no doubt that he could have succeeded in any number of other occupations. Despite the extra demands brought about by Dad's illness, he had always kept up to speed with his schoolwork, constantly outscoring his namesake, and distant cousin, at the other side of the bridge. That lad is now one of the top men in the largest accountancy firm in town. He is married to a teacher, with a son and two daughters—all now in secondary school. He drives a flashy BMW and has built a veritable mansion beside his mother's house. He continues to farm on a part-time basis, buying in and fattening about twenty bullocks each summer.

The rain has stopped. She winds the line of drying clothes from the shelter of the redundant hayshed to the hazy sunlight of the yard. Not for the first time, she marvels at his ingenuity in conceiving such an apparatus. His invention—yes, invention is the correct word—means that she can transfer a full wash from the cover of the shed to the fresh air without having to unpeg a single garment. It had been his idea to combine a series of pulleys, rollers and cogs, a length of nylon twine, and the winch wheel and handle from the obsolete hay cart, to devise a user-friendly, all-weather clothesline. Yes, with his brain he could hold his own with a teacher. God knows, he could buy and sell some of the dul amús she'd had to contend with in her schooldays. It would be a relief to see him settled, to know that he would have a future and that the family name would survive through another generation.

Something small and white erupts from within the depths of the shed and flashes past her, closely followed by the tabby farm cat. It's only when Sal, after a pirouetting leap in the air, sets off in pursuit at a jauntily exaggerated trot that she realises the truth. Typical, she hisses to herself, it wouldn't be the first time you've kept a kitten or a pup hidden until it was too late for me to do anything about it… Still, for more than ten minutes, she watches the antics of Sal as the dog tries to join in the cats' play. She suddenly recalls the day when Mam had explained that while a mother cat will rarely join in the rough and tumble of her brood, she will always play with a lone kitten. How long ago had that been; thirty-five, forty, or more likely, forty-five years? Yet, until now, she has never witnessed such an event. At the reminder pips of her phone, she lets out a long sigh. It's time she was getting ready.

Her head in a spin, she unlocks the red Octavia. Had the doctor really said those words? After weeks of preparing for a death sentence, had she been granted a new lease on life? A hysterectomy is a small price to pay, she affirms, studying her reflection in the rearview mirror. Now that her hair won't be falling out, she can make an appointment at the salon—have a proper colour put in. On impulse, she relocks the car and strides towards the Chinese take-away. It will make a nice change for him, too—particularly after a few pints.

"What are you doing here? I thought you'd be in the pub…" He is standing by the takeaway doorway, an aromatic carrier bag dangling from his left hand.

"No. Jim-the forge offered me a lift. We did all right with the calves, so I said I'd give you a break from cooking. Will I tell Jim to work away?"

She wants to tell him, but as she hadn't shared her anxiety, neither can she share her relief. She hopes he won't ask why she has dressed up. He doesn't but suggests they might invest in a Belgian Blue bull after the Simmental has completed next year's duties.

She serves the reheated meal when he returns from reuniting the calf-less cows with the rest of the herd. Afterwards, he expands on the benefits of introducing Belgian Blue blood to their stock and poses the possibility of buying a pedigree heifer or two to hasten the process.

"You seem distracted. Anything wrong?" Not receiving a response, he calls her by name.

"What? No… sorry, I… I was just thinking. You know, about new blood. I was thinking about getting a few pullets…"

"Ah, I knew you'd get tired of the supermarket eggs…"

"No… yes. Would you have a chat with your friend… you know, at the farmers' market?"

"Me? What do I know about chickens? I wouldn't know a broiler from a bantam."

"But she knows…"

"Yeah, but if I bring home a flock of cockerels, you'll…"

"Look, it's time you started making your own decisions: either you trust her or you don't."

She watches him encourage Sal into the cab of the tractor and drive towards the passage that leads to the mountain commonage where their sheep graze. He'll be gathering the flock in a week or so, separating the lambs from their mothers, and then deciding which ewe lambs will go to market along with the wethers. Then it will be time to reintroduce the rams to the flock, and the whole cycle will be start over again. She goes to his room and pilfers a cigarette from his secret stash. She wonders if he knows that she knows… if he has noticed her occasional thefts. God knows, she had warned him often enough throughout his teens, even into his twenties. He should be well aware of the dangers by now. She slips silently out to the silent yard before lighting up, and she then exhales with a long sigh.

She retires to her room after watching the main TV news and weather forecast, leaving him engrossed in one of his wildlife documentaries.

She is still flitting through her magazine when she hears his knock.

"What is it?" she asks. "Tonight isn't that cold."

"No," he says. Then, after a pause, adds, "'tisn't the cold; 'tis the company."

Over by the Coliseum

R. Bratten Weiss

You are looking for a trashcan for your empty paper cup,
but instead you find a man dressed as a Pharaoh,
with a tiny Etruscan smile on his gilded face,
and another man dressed as a centurion, shouting
trips for two, trips for two, as the tourists pass by,
and another man dressed as your ex-lover, taking
a selfie with the ruined Empire behind him, on a stick.

Oh baby, you say to him, I remember how you never
went down smooth and sweet, how you never even held
your toy sword against my throat, or buried me down
in your playground pyramid, with scarabs on my eyes.

He doesn't listen, he's trapped in a selfie, head on a
plinth, and little black and gold lizards flicker across
his smile. Whatever it was he knew, he
never told you. The lizards are crawling down into
his throat now, and nearby the play centurion holds
his toy sword against the lily throat of a rich-girl bride.

When you find the trashcan at last you crumple up
the cup with the lipstick stains, you crumple up
everything, you walk on into the cities of the dead.

Night Watch

Sharon J. Wishnow

Luke wagged his long red-furred tail as I scratched that special silky spot where his ear met his head. He rested on his favorite spot on the couch, his triangle head on my lap.

"Still feels good boy, doesn't it?" I cooed to him. His chocolate brown eyes were half closed in an almost human expression of contentment. He bumped his cold wet nose underneath my hand, an implied request to stroke him. I let the silky fur bunch between my fingers and scratched the length of his back, feeling the vertebrae poke under my palm. His once muscular body, shiny penny coat, now fur and bones. I was thanked with another hearty tail thump.

We planned on giving Reese a dog for this sixth birthday. He had begged for a dog for as long as he could talk. We did our research and learned Irish setters were loyal companions and good with children. The time was right, and the dog would be a good distraction for him.

Reese was worried about his first day of first grade, clinging to me as if some calamity was imminent if we were separated. His nightmares and panic attacks were unpredictable. I read child development books and scanned the Internet for articles on transitioning to school. Everything assured me this was a development phase and to stay strong. A friend who had similar issues with her daughter suggested a dog would help, give him something to concentrate on, calm him down, and show him that he could make good decisions.

As the first day approached, Reese complained of body aches. "He's nervous." I said to Bill. "He's so wound up he's making himself sick." The aches came with a fever and lethargy. Off we went to the pediatrician. Instead of a first-grade boy and his dog, we got a boy and his cancer.

For all of his fears, Reese was the mortar keeping our spirits and hopes from crumbling. The one constant about treatment was boredom. "A dog would keep me company," he said. He wasn't giving up on his dream.

Bill and I went back and forth about the puppy while Reese was in treatment. "A puppy is too much work right now." Bill, always logical and practical, was right. But I was full of emotions.

"Maybe, we could get an older dog." I said.

He shook his head and brushed his hand across my cheek. "I want to give him the world too, but we're already wrung out."

I nodded but whispered to Reese that there would be a dog, soon. I never said the unspoken, when you're better, because I believed if I said it out loud, maybe it wouldn't happen.

Eighteen months later, we had a bright, happy Irish setter puppy to match the boundless newfound energy of our child, now in remission from leukemia. Our home was overflowing with light and hope.

The puppy skidded across the tile floor in a scritch-scratch frenzy and a high-pitched yelp, fighting his own too-big paws, nails trying and failing to take purchase. Reese laughed, his whole body shook, a sound I had never heard. It was an expulsion of air, a clearing of the sickness from this body. The leukemia had no place to hold onto inside. Bill and I laughed too. All three of us sat on the floor, calling to the dog to see which way he'd chose.

"What should we call him?" Bill said.

"Luke," Reese said and scratched the puppy's ears. "For leukemia."

The tile floor felt cold, like a specter had placed an invisible finger at the edge, freezing it over like a pond in winter.

"Are you sure?" Bill said, seeing the horror cross my face.

Reese nodded without meeting our gaze. "I'm better, that's why you let me have him. I have leukemia to thank for him."

It was odd eight-year-old logic. It had been two years of leukemia, the leukemia, the cancer, call it what it was. I wasn't thanking it for anything, only for it being gone.

The boy grew and his dog grew, constant playmates, best friends, equally matched in their energy, one always chasing the other. Two months before Reese turned ten, Luke began to whimper, he walked around the house at night, and cried when Reese was at school.

"What's wrong, boy?" I ran my hands over him, looking for burrs or ticks, something to explain his change. I took him to the vet, but he was fine.

Reese changed too, sleeping longer and turning up his nose at hot dogs, potato chips, and strawberry ice cream.

"Seriously, not even ice cream?" I said one day. "Is everything okay at school?" Middle schoolers could be cruel. Reese was small and thin for his age. I knew one boy, Seth, had picked on him in the past.

I let it go. Weeks later, Luke pounced on our bed in the middle of the night and snatched the blanket from us.

"Get down, boy." Bill pushed the dog off the bed, annoyed by the 2:00 am dog alarm. Luke rebounded with more energy and let out one clear bark. I sat up with a start.

"Bill, it's Reese."

I scrambled out of bed with Luke running ahead to Reese's room. The blankets and sheets had been kicked to the floor. He lay in a fetal position, small and exposed. Light from the streetlamp shone through the window blinds, slicing his body into horizontal slits. I didn't need to touch him to know he had a fever. It wasn't the flu.

"The dog knew." I cried in Bill's arms when we got the news from the oncologist. "He knew weeks ago. Why didn't I take Reese to the doctor? I took Luke to the vet instead. I'm a horrible mother."

I stayed by Reese's side for the next three weeks and slept in his hospital room. When I came home, I discovered that Luke had taken my spot on the bed next to Bill. I couldn't be mad, they needed each other while we were gone. As soon as Reese came home, Luke returned to his regular perch at the end of Reese's bed, the night-watch dog. I slept better knowing he was there.

Reese's recovery from the relapse was slow. I'd watch from the kitchen window as he sat in a lawn chair and threw a ball for Luke, who was more than happy to chase anything, no matter the time of day. Luke had dug a hole under part of our fence to reach the squirrel-filled woods. The furry gray rodents mocked him from their tall perches. He'd pace the fence line, long nose pointed skyward, and let out a conversation of yips, snarls, and barks of frustration. Reese would call to him and the dog would look over, wanting to obey his master, throw a final backward glance to the woods, and trot over.

Reese died eighteen months later. A loud silence and a blackness deeper than a coal mine. Bill and I would take long, silent hikes in the woods. Luke lead the way and circled back to make sure we kept up.

We lost our connection, our happiness, and talked about divorce. We weren't the first couple to lose a child and lose a marriage. It wasn't that we didn't love each other. We couldn't bear the pain we each felt. Grief counseling didn't help. A suggested vacation to the Bahamas was a temporary tonic until we came home. The house remained empty. Cruel reminders accosted us in the form of straggling medical bills. I'd wait on hold for some efficient robot-sounding human at the insurance company who assured me he was there to answer any questions. "My son is dead, and you are sending me bills that I'm not responsible for paying." That was usually met with an intake of breath and silence, followed by an apology and the problem being resolved.

We sat one night and talked about our split. We agreed to sell the house, an unspoken understanding there were too many ghosts lurking everywhere. Neither of us wanted to live with the haunting. Next came the division of furniture, dishes, artwork, electronics, and a laugh over unused and senseless wedding gifts tarnished in the basement. Then there was Luke. Neither of us could claim him. He wasn't my dog or Bill's dog. He was Reese's dog and a dog that belonged to himself. I had played with the idea of just opening the back fence and letting him be free to frolic with the squirrels. He sat by our side during that discussion, looking casually from one of us to the other. He thumped his tail, hearing his name. That thump was like a trumpet blast. An unexpected sound of happiness and neediness in our silence. He needed us, we needed him.

Bill and I shared a bed that night, the first time in six months. Luke in the middle, a neutral party policing a treaty. Eventually we relegated him to the floor and found our way back to each other. Two years later, Mandy was born. We think she may be Luke's daughter, her hair is a shade lighter than his fur. To Reese, Luke was a twin sibling; to Mandy he was an older brother. He put up with her constant toddler tugs at his ears and tail and attempts to ride him. He was rewarded for his patience by the fists full of Cheerios she could never hold onto long enough to eat. He'd vacuum up her crumbs as she explored her world and wait patiently under her highchair. She'd happily toss her meals over the side and laugh and clap at his mid-air gulping.

"Lukey smells bad." Mandy patted the dog's head with an exaggerated pump of her palm. Now four years old, she understood that she needed to be gentle with the dog.

"Maybe he needs another bubble bath." I grabbed her and blew a raspberry in the soft spot between her shoulder and neck. She squirmed and giggled and let me pull her up onto the couch next to me.

"What are you and Daddy doing today?" I refastened a slipped butterfly-shaped clip in her hair.

"I'm going to ride my bike!"

"Are you now?" Bill had been eager for Mandy to learn to ride. Reese had never been interested.

"Will you come watch?"

"As soon as Luke takes his nap."

"Bye, stinky Lukey." She patted his head and was rewarded by a tail thump.

Stinky Lukey was right. I had bathed him yesterday and even he was happy to escape the smell. He was dying, and a malodorous cloud was shedding off him, from his fur to his stale breath. He was in Addison crisis. His kidneys were shutting down, and he shook as if in a constant north wind. I spent hours of my days on the couch with him. We had covered a foam egg crate bed pad with terry cloth and let him lie on the couch. At first, he would crawl onto my lap and any attempt I made to move made him whimper. We quickly developed a boundary. He would rest his head on my lap, allowing me to shift and stretch. He demanded constant attention like a sick child. I was in no position to say no, neither was Bill.

"Mandy and I are going to take him outside." Bill swung Mandy by her arms, and she landed gently on a chair. He picked up Luke, cradled him in his arms, kissed him on his head, and went outside. I stood, stretched, and did a quick round of chores, relishing the free time. Too soon, I heard the back door slam shut and, "Good boy, Lukey!" from Mandy.

"Ready for this boy?" Bill shook a bottle of pills. Luke responded with a soft bark, doggy Xanax. It kept him calm as he worked on dying. I took Xanax too, popped them dry like Tic Tacs. The only difference was Luke had his wrapped in a piece of American cheese.

"He's back." Bill said.

"Me too!" Mandy said.

My eyes took in Mandy sitting on Bill's shoulders trying to touch the ceiling fan with her hands. Luke was small in his arms, more fur than dog.

"Bill." I laughed. "You're going to hurt your back carrying the whole family."

"Mandy weighs more than Luke these days."

The reality crushed me and I turned to straighten the towels on the couch for him. The Xanax would make him sleep and I would head out to see Mandy on her bike.

"Mia, Mia," Bill shook my shoulder. I had fallen asleep on the couch, Luke's nose resting on my feet. The TV whispered the jokes of a late-night talk show host and his guest. "Come to bed, it's past eleven."

"Oh, okay. Take Luke."

"He's sleeping, he can stay here tonight."

I shook my head. I wasn't leaving him.

Bill crouched beside my head, "It's time to let him go. The vet said anytime we were ready."

I pushed myself up, now fully awake and reached out to pet Luke.

Bill stopped my hand. "Don't, you'll wake him."

"It's not time. He's not in pain. I didn't put Reese down." I saw the words come out of my mouth like vapor on a freezing morning, hot with regret.

Bill turned and left.

"I didn't mean that like it sounded."

He whipped back, "You don't get to own all the world's sadness. It's time you got off that damned couch with that damned dog and became a person again."

I slid to the floor, the tears followed. "He's all I have left of Reese. He holds his soul. He's not just a damned dog. Where would we be without him?"

My hulk of a husband started to speak, stuttering on his own biting words, but never releasing them. They were replaced with his usual logic. "One more week, we'll see how he is, and you come to bed now and leave him be."

I stopped in Mandy's room and rested beside her. Her breaths were clear and regular, her skin warm but not feverish. She smelled like strawberries from her shampoo. A slight smile played on her lips. I tucked her chubby arm under the blanket. She had all the vitality and strength that Reese had lost, maybe all that he never had. I worried constantly that a switch in her would flip and we would live the nightmare again. The pediatrician assured me that her chances of getting leukemia were no higher because of Reese. I kissed her cheek and backed out of her room. I stopped at the top of the stairs, listening for Luke, a change in breathing, a whimper. My mommy ears extended to him as well. He was quiet, a gift he had given me, and I went to bed. I turned a cold shoulder to Bill, our backs to each other, another brokered truce because of Luke. All allies have setbacks, I mused, and fell asleep.

The week passed and Luke did change. He got off the couch one morning and padded outside to watch Mandy in the backyard.

"Lukey, come join the tea party!"

Mandy had set the picnic table with plastic teacups for a menagerie of her favorite stuffed animals. Luke wasn't interested in the party, even turning his nose away from an offered real cookie.

I watched from the kitchen window, remembering Luke playing with Reese. He hefted his shaking body over to the fence and pointed his nose to the forest. He got a whiff of his old nemeses, the squirrels, and a long-forgotten conversation of yips, snarls, and barks was launched over the fence.

Luke refused to come inside. Bill reached to lift him, and he squirmed with more energy than we had seen in weeks.

"Okay boy, you can stay in the yard if you want." Bill shrugged.

I crouched low to rub his head. It was a warm night. I brought out a bowl of water and some food. We sat with him under the moon, swinging back and forth in a glider.

"Which is the dog star?"

Bill looked up. "I have no idea."

His seriousness made us laugh, that turned into an uncontrollable fit. A release of emotions and escape.

When I woke in the morning, Bill was lying next to Luke on the ground, stroking that long feathery penny-red fur and talking softly. I knew he was gone. I closed my eyes to give him his private moment to say goodbye. To let go of Reese's soul, to let go.

Carnival Evening
Taunja Thomson

It is a carnival evening—
iron sky has drawn its tent
of clouds
overhead and topped it
with moon.
Trees stand as poles
holding all together
with brittle fingers.
You and I stroll
inside the ring
of dark green
that stretches
for miles
and miles—
there are no wires
no knockabouts
no calliopes
no candy pitches
after all these years
just dusk
folding us softly
into its side.

Today I Bought New Cutlery
Jack Mackey

a whole set
to replace the crap I bought when I first moved out.
It reminded me of the time we bought
our first knives and forks and spoons,
two of each, all we needed
for that upstairs furnished flat
with ratty carpet and cockroaches.
I think we went to Woolworths
in some rundown strip mall outside D.C.,
on a rainy Friday night in mid-September,
after our passion had burst through spring and flattened
summer,
oblivious then to loan payments and slow leaking tires,
now we had real dinner times to consider.
We had decided to settle in for a while,
clutching our recent sheepskins and
carrying our casual first creation, beating quietly.

Earlier in the day, I carried out the trash
that contained plastic, paper, crystal, silver,
I uncovered the new diary you gave me that I did not keep,
would not keep,
that I had forgotten, lying
still secure in its blankness in the dumpster, longing
to be forgotten again,
to be re-covered, deep, in a landfill.

I found the spoon we used to make instant coffee,
all we ever drank for years,
never committing the time to brew anything.
I have a small scar over my eye from the fork,
the bent one you threw at me
on the cluttered night when I told you.

After I left we had to find a way
to bury the past without burying everything.
When I see you now
your face shines with the pain of what we lost –
the heart we thought would thump forever –
and the sorrow of eating alone.

First Love

James M. LeCuyer

I was depressingly unsuccessful with girls when I was in middle school. For years, through the tenth grade, I had terrible acne on my face and deep boils on my back. I had no experience with girls, no girls my age in my family. Yet I desired them as a bee might a flower, something necessary and sweet but entirely different than me, beautiful creatures to which I was drawn but could never have, not even as a simple insect might, coating myself in their essence. I was afraid of girls even as I fantasized about them. Many boys my age boasted of having two or three. But some must be terrible liars.

In deepest privacy I used a magnifying glass to stare at photos in Sunbather magazines that featured nude volleyball-playing females with breasts and nipples and dark patches between their legs. I imagined a beautiful girl moaning in my eager ear, "Oh, Jim" as I caressed her. I was quite innocently perverted. Disappointed too. As my magnifying glass wavered up and down, the nipples I so desired would dissolve into newsprint dots.

Even after infinite acne treatments from trained nurses not much older than me torturing my pride and back and face with tiny spears with hooks, and minute circular knives to dig out exploding boils, and after a vile diet that excluded bacon and Milky Ways and even good old healthy-for-you milk, a diet that limited me to such delicacies as eggs fried only in salt, and after my complexion had mostly cleared, even then I might blush horribly if left alone with a girl, and I would have no luck. I might spend days reading about and rehearsing subjects that I thought a particular girl might be interested in, like poetry, and talk a girl's ear off the first time I walked with her down a hall, then have nothing more to say the second time I saw her. I'd merely turn red with embarrassment if, as usually happened, neither of us had much to say.

The very intensity of my desire for girls kept me from touching them intimately. I knew how horribly sexual my thoughts were, and I felt they must shine from me like blinking neon signs. Like great horns. Like pimples. Zits flashing. Sex. Sex. Sex.

I envied the football players, the black-leathered rebels, the suave, quiet spoken high school Romeos who had the most beautiful girls in school hanging on them, girls I lusted after and would have given an arm or a whole foot if they would only hang on my neck in the same fashion. I was short and skinny, and, once you looked past my pimples, more feminine in features than masculine with my innocent wide eyes that I tried to half shut in a mean Humphrey Bogart manner, trying to look as if I were older and tough as nails, despite my sweet face.

My friend Bobby would ask, "What the hell's wrong with you. Are you angry at something?"

"No," I'd say, readjusting my mean eyes ever so slightly, perhaps lifting my eyebrows. "Everything copacetic, man." Tough to the bone.

My aunts had long ago told me I was "cute as a button," and that I'd "one day" be a "woman killer," so I had patient hope that all of a sudden, I'd blossom into Cary Grant handsome. Girls would flock about, even fight over me. I'd learn to be smooth.

"I'm sorry," I would someday say as I gently shook the excess girls free. "P'raps tomorrow."

When I was twelve and thirteen, after my parents left for work, I would sometimes wrap my head in my mother's shawl so my face shone forth as a perfect oval, and stare at my full, lipsticked, red lips in her dresser mirror, thinking I'd make a lovely girl. I would be Jamie. Then I'd shake off the shawl, narrow my eyes, and stick one of my father's cigarettes in my sucked-in thin, sardonic lips, and see the hardboiled detective face of my future. Or I'd take a piece of charcoal and darken my pink cheeks and become a threatening hood, a James Cagney, a cool Alan Ladd. Yeh. Okay. People would talk to me and I'd say nothing. Only my eyes might tighten as if I were about to shoot them for speaking in my presence.

But, apart from one Halloween handholding in a vampire movie and one horribly embarrassing dance party in which I refused to dance with or speak to my date, the exquisitely beautiful Charlene, (had asked me on a dare from her friends, I found out), I had little personal contact with girls until the eleventh grade. I had an adult cousin, Betty, whom I loved and lusted after, but no young girls in my immediate family.

If I'd only known a few and understood how small minded even a very desirable girl could be, I might have saved myself much anguish. I didn't know that some beautiful girls could be as self-centered as a toad inside. Or that they might feel shy around me. I didn't know that many suffered from pimples, too. Just because I was attracted to a girl, didn't mean she was kind and intelligent and loving. I did think girls were less mean and disgusting than boys. I imagined I would meet a pure all-around inside-and-out beautiful girl, one I could adore. I listed the qualities she had to have, fine cheekbones for example, delicate ankles. She would like to read. She'd want to put her arms around my neck and hang on me. She'd be perfect. Meanwhile, I'd accept almost any girl at all.

I could write a little, so I found a niche on our school newspaper, The Blue and White. I spent after school hours hiding out behind a typewriter, writing a sports column or a feature story. I disguised myself as a student. Our paper came out daily. We even had our own hot-type printing press. Class work and newspaper work kept me busier than my thoughts, though at night I was dreadfully lonely.

I hated going home. I would stay at school until Mr. Robert, the journalism instructor, would send me out into the world at five or so, when he closed up. I'd hurry home and crawl into bed to avoid the ugly, explosive silence that lay between my parents. I was well on my hermit's path at sixteen, long after all other boys seemingly not only had girlfriends but had had infinite sexual experiences—girls who "went down" on them or would "go all the way."

I wondered how it would be to enter a monastery and devote myself to God, for it was plain I was never going to be suave, charming, and witty. Certainly not until I was sixty or seventy. Not even God would want me, for I had no religious beliefs at all.

My face was scarred with pimple holes and pimples that bloomed with every perfumed breeze from a nearby girl, no matter how casual I tried to be. Sunbather magazines would have to do, but none of the naked women there met my standards. They were fat, or saggy, or too thin. And they were only newspaper dots.

I did have one friend who was female, but only an odd girl, Claudette, a sad-eyed female who was not even on the staff of the paper but who used to come in and play around a bit with me in journalism after school. All very innocent. She'd ball up a newspaper and pitch it at me, and I'd swing a ruler and hit it or miss it, and we'd laugh together. She came in often, and I grew used to her. She was popular among her girlfriends, but her crooked nose and slightly weak chin put her out of the competition for available sports heroes. I thought she was not interested in me as a boyfriend nor did I see her as my ideal female, so I forgot to lust after her. We became pals.

Dick, my old neighborhood friend who was two years ahead of me, had rushed a fraternity at UCLA. A fraternity at a university seemed like a dream story, something from a Hollywood film. He invited me to a party at Delta Tau Delta.

He said, "You'll need to drive, there are no buses nearby, and you'll have to bring a girlfriend. Couples only." He said these things as if they were commonplace, though the only times I'd ever driven any car was when my father was sitting next to me, and I had only a lustful prayer for a girlfriend. There was, of course, Claudette. But we only knew each other from fooling around after school in journalism.

I wanted to go to that party. I really wanted to go. I didn't know any other girls. I floated the party idea out in space near her to see what might happen.

I said, "I have a chance to go to a fraternity party at UCLA. Do you know any girls who might like to go with me?" I cleverly said it so she wouldn't feel I was asking her. Not that I didn't want her to go, but I didn't want her to think I was trapping her, and I certainly didn't want her to flat out refuse. That would have been devastating, for I really enjoyed our little games after school, batting balls of paper, chasing each other around desks. I didn't want to chase her off.

"I wouldn't mind going," she said. "I'd love it."

I had no words for how I felt. I felt panic. Had I actually asked her? I had. I knew I had. I knew what I was doing as I did it. But I wanted to give her an out. Maybe she really did know someone else. But who? She had some pretty undesirable girlfriends. But now she wanted to go, and now I might have to spend the whole evening with her, talking about what? What were girls interested in, anyway?

I tried to think of her as a girlfriend. Her eyes were a startling shade of copper. She was petite but shapely, if a little plain. But she had unfortunate cocker spaniel cheeks and nose, sort of squashed, and a naturally mournful expression. But we were such friends that I barely thought of her in the same way I thought of the multitude of unavailable girls like Charlene. And I'd grown used to her features, even fond of them. Maybe looks didn't matter. Who was I, with my volcanic face, to be choosy?

One of the boys, a basketball player, on the Blue and White journalism staff called Claudette a puppy dog, and I "accidentally" spilled hot coffee on his shirt.

"Sorry, sorry," I'd said.

He said, "You scorched me. You wrecked my polo shirt!"

Good, I thought.

As soon as Claudette said she herself wanted to go, I immediately began to back away. I needed a quick out. I said. "I don't know if I can get my father's car."

"Oh, would you?" she said eagerly, apparently assuming I had said I expected to get the car. "That's lovely. I've always wanted to go to a fraternity party." She was so pleased. She balled up several newspapers and started throwing them at me, bouncing them off my head like snowballs. I chased her around the room throwing paper airplanes I made on the run, both of us screaming until Mr. Robert came out of his little office and screamed a most un-Robert-like, "QUIET!"

I ran the idea past my father. I wanted him to say no. "I don't suppose you'll let me drive your car on a date."

My father looked at me as if a tree or a cloud had just spoken to him. To the best of his knowledge, I had absolutely no interest in girls. I'd never said a word about them, or even looked at them. I'd never brought one around. He asked me occasionally if I had a girlfriend at school, and I always shook my head in disgust, not at the idea of me having a girlfriend, but at his snooping into my privacy. Of course, he didn't know that. He had no idea about my fantasies, my stash of Sunbather magazines I hid under my tennis shoes in the closet, the secret use I made of my magnifying glass. He was my father after all. What could a father know of sex? I certainly didn't want to know anything at all about his thoughts on this matter.

"It's just a girl I know from school," I said, "and I guess it wouldn't be legal for me to drive alone, so I don't suppose you could lend it."

He was sitting on our one overstuffed chair in the front room in his big red bathrobe after a shower, reading the Herald-Examiner, some pages spread out on the rug. He nodded his head in a particularly irritating manner, slowly, as if pondering the non-request I'd made. He was both clean and sober, a miracle. Black hairs covered his milk-white body. When home, he drank great amounts of cheap wine, while my mother barricaded herself in her locked bedroom. I didn't particularly like him, and I didn't know anyone who did. He wasn't home much, so we endured each other.

When he didn't say anything, I turned to leave the room. I'd tell Claudette no, maybe some other time, sorry I'd mentioned anything to her. I'd hate to disappoint her, but she was just a friend who happened to be a girl.

But a friend who was a girl! Well. It came to me as a kind of illumination. She'd snuck up on me. A girl could theoretically be a friend, as much as a boy might. A girlfriend. Now that I might get her, I didn't know if I wanted this particular one. I'd never had a real girlfriend, not since the innocent days of the third grade, anyway, when I'd had three who claimed they were my girlfriends, though I'd only talked to them on the schoolyard. I hadn't wanted them, and I ignored them as much as possible when I found out what they were saying about me.

As I was about to leave the room, my father said, "Why not?"

"Why not what?"

"You can take the car."

I'd been so caught up in excusing myself to Claudette, I'd almost forgotten I'd asked him for the car. I started to argue with him.

"The car?"

"Yes," he said. "Who's the girl?"

The car. He meant I could drive it on my own, and I could go to the party, but I would have to take Claudette.

"A friend on the newspaper, a dumb girl named Claudette."

He looked at me and nodded as if he wisely understood everything. I hated that look. I hated asking my parents for anything, and wouldn't have, except, because of Claudette, I'd had to ask him, certain it was totally impossible. I expected his no, and that would be my excuse, and I'd tell Claudette no, and we could go on the rest of our high school lives throwing paper wads at each other.

"You're a good driver," he said. "I don't see why not. I drove a Model A when I was your age. You drive well. If you get stopped, that'll be a good lesson for you, and I'll say I had nothing to do with it. You'll be on your own. Get it?" These were the most words he'd said to me in months.

Here he was saying yes, and suddenly I thought of Claudette's white sweater that she wore on cold winter days, and how she filled it out. I'd been ambushed, certainly not by Claudette but by something I didn't comprehend, a drop of rain from an innocent little white cloud.

"You'll need some money," he said.

"No, I won't," I said. I didn't, either. I had nearly two hundred dollars hidden in L. Frank Baum's The Scarecrow of Oz. I'd been saving odds and ends of money, some of which I stole from him when he was passed out. I'd wanted a ten-speed English Racer, but now a bike seemed childish. A car… I thought of the possibilities, the instant fame I'd achieve, the girls I could drive around. A car was the answer. Late night cruising. Pizza. Zuma Beach. Stardom. Not yet a star, but on the road to the Emerald City.

There were a few confused moments as I waited for my father's final words. He might rescind his agreement. It wasn't like him to say yes to such a risky thing. I might be arrested. I might wreck the car. What if it had a flat tire?

Some people want something so much that they overcome all obstacles by sheer persistence. Not me. My friend Bobby would push his stern father to a breaking point, and even take a smack to get what he wanted. I never asked for anything, except to remain as unknown as possible to my father. I wondered how I'd managed to ask him for the car. It was an act of courage equivalent, in itself, to going over the top and charging the enemy.

I'd asked not exactly because of the fraternity party, and definitely not for a date with Claudette, but because I was a wishy washy idiot and had more or less promised Claudette I would ask him, and I was a good boy and could imagine the number of lies I'd have to tell her if I didn't. And while I was a good liar, if pushed hard, as my mother sometimes did, I'd have to confess.

"What did he say?" She'd look at me with her expectant, metallic eyes. I'd have to respond clearly. A mumble wouldn't do. She had a way of pinning me down. My general technique for asking for something was to hint at it, and let it go if I didn't get it. Not Claudette. She was very nice, but she demanded answers. I might think I was smarter, but she was the treasurer and recording secretary of the Junior Class, and one of the main organizers of the Senior Prom.

No! I thought, with dread. The Senior Prom! One date and you were engaged to be married. But wouldn't that be nice? A lovely naked girl to sleep next to, all legal and just waiting there every night. But Claudette?

My father checked me out on his car, an ancient navy blue 1941 Chevy Coupe with one of the first ever automatic transmissions, sort of a wreck, but functional. I'd driven it with him or with my mother several times, so I knew the car. He had me drive to UCLA and back without saying a word, and he made me nervous, but I didn't make any serious screwups.

When I told Claudette about the car, she was overjoyed. She hugged me and kissed me on the cheek. My pimply cheek. Her bosom was, for a delicious moment, pressed against my chest. We'd have to talk about this on the phone, she told me. I worried about that too, for I never had much to say to anyone on the phone. I had to see them and watch their faces for changing moods before I knew what to say. Even then, I didn't say much. I responded to questions. But my general silence didn't bother her at all. She had plenty to say.

There was still a chance her parents wouldn't let her go, but she said I wasn't to worry about that.

"That's okay," I said. "If this doesn't work, we can go to something else in a few weeks."

"Oh no," she said. "Don't worry. We're going to this party this time."

She had a week to work the parents over, and by the day of the party, they were ready to buy her a new car, a house, anything. So, she told me on the phone, lowering her voice. The father, who was French, had sworn at her until he hadn't the energy to whisper. Then the mother, a devout Catholic, had prayed in French, and life went on. Claudette gave me a daily account of her progress, a view of a family entirely different than mine. And what did I know of this girl? It didn't matter. I'd begun to desire her. I'd shifted my thoughts of what a dream girl might be, just a little.

When I picked up Claudette, I had on a new, white shirt, khaki slacks, and a new pair of black penny loafers. My mother had bought them for me. My father had told her about my date. I was hopelessly embarrassed by their interest in my private life.

I felt so little like myself in those clothes I could have laughed. Before I left for Claudette's house, I posed in front of the bathroom mirror and made silly faces, flexed my arms, grabbed my crotch. What I was doing I had no idea.

And I had almost as little idea what to expect at a fraternity party. Dick had said, "Watch out for the orange juice. They use lab alcohol and you can't taste it."

I told Claudette, but she was much more sophisticated than I was about parties, and alcohol, and fraternity boys. She had girlfriends who'd told her all about them, how the parties could get wild, when to be friendly and when to get out fast. I confessed to her I couldn't dance because I didn't know the first thing about it and had only gone to one dance and had failed miserably. That was quite a confession for me. I felt safe telling her because she was a friend and we'd told each other many secrets. She had confessed that boys often ignored her, that she knew she was not beautiful, but I assured her she was just fine

"Oh," she said mysteriously. "We heard about that dance." I blushed. I realized that things I thought hidden in the past had been discussed by girls at school. "But don't worry,'" she said, I'll teach you. Dancing is simple."

The Delta Tau Delta House on Euclid was built up on a hill, an old-fashioned building with two fake Greek pillars holding up a porch roof over the front door. Inside there was a great, yelling crowd, pounding music from a small band, boys holding beer cans, girls milling about, some looking up into the eyes of older boys. I found Dick and introduced him to Claudette. He looked at her approvingly.

"Hey, not bad," he said, his palm curling over his own chest when she looked away. It was obvious what he meant. I resented his crude interest in her chest.

But this was the first time I'd ever thought she might be attractive to others, even if in an odd sort of way. She was small, only five two, but her bosom amply filled her lovely white, angora sweater.

We were twins in white and tan. She wore bobby sox and a pleated copper colored skirt that matched her eyes. I had on my white shirt and tan slacks. She smelled good, like lemons. Around us swirled a mass of men and women, all older than we were, and

Claudette and I clung to each other, two knowns in a mass of unknowns.

Dick was responsible for snacks and party management, so we lost him right away. I could feel Claudette's breasts hot against my arm. We got drinks from a bar decorated with palm fronds out on the back volleyball court. The drinks were free, and no one asked how old we were. Palm frond cabanas lined the court, and torches flamed from two cement volleyball posts. All very exotic.

"Are you rushing?" said a young guy possibly not much older than me.

"I'm just here as a friend."

"Right," he said. "I'm a friend too, but I'm rushing the Delts anyway."

I wasn't sure what he meant, but Claudette said rushing meant he wanted to join the fraternity.

We danced. We actually danced. I relaxed into it. I had one screwdriver, and Claudette had a glass of wine. We were both sixteen. It was heavenly. It was a warm house, fleshy with sensuality, girls almost popping out of their bras. The band inside played Dixieland, and another band outside in one corner of the volleyball court played slow dance music. We danced to Glenn Miller and Count Basie and Duke Ellington, a lot of old stuff, but perfect for dancing slow. I never felt closer to anyone than I did with Claudette on that night. If I lost the rhythm, she would laugh and I would grin like a clown.

We stayed until eleven, until Claudette said she hated to say it but she better get back before midnight, and she was worried about the alcohol. I'd just gulped down the last of my fourth screwdriver. I was never happier. I wanted to touch her everywhere. I ran my hands all over her hips and the rising curve of her buttocks as we danced. I had a hard-on and let it touch her thigh, and she just snuggled up closer. I thought I could do anything if I just had the courage to try, and I was filled with heroics, let me take on the world. First, let me undress Claudette.

On the drive back, the fourth screwdriver started to hit home runs, and all the lights swirled double, out of focus. Lab alcohol.

I couldn't blink the images together. I had to guess when to stop, how to accelerate slowly and carefully, how to keep the white line off to my left and stay steady on the road. It was a game. I wasn't exactly there.

"You okay?" she asked.

"Sure. Sure. Fine." But I was spacing out at each stoplight, and she had to poke me to get me going.

I laughed sneakily, my upper lip drooped down over my lower. Every movement was slow and thought out in advance, though my mouth and feet and hands were trying to operate on their own. I knew if I were to be stopped by a cop, I'd be hauled off, the world spinning into a cell, my father laughing at me.

Just outside Claudette's house I parked and reached for her. She was completely ready for anything, and though I had no experience with women to speak of, I knew we could go very far. I closed my eyes, thinking this is how you kiss, nose tipped to one side, my first parked-in-a-car romantic kiss. But as soon as I closed my eyes the world started to spiral up into the warm night sky, right through the roof of the car. Nebulae and galaxies and suns and dark stars. I opened my eyes and saw Claudette's pursed lips whirl past me. I flung my lips at hers but landed only for the briefest instant.

"Excuse me," I said, as I turned from her, rolled down the window, and vomited an orangish sour-smelling fluid with undigested bits of something green. I was horrified. Claudette screamed, ran into her house, and slammed her door, the chain clanging behind her. Our first kiss and I'd vomited. I zig-zagged after her and banged on the door.

"It's not you," I yelled at her shadow behind the thick panes of glass. "It's the screwdrivers." I desperately wanted her to know it wasn't her fault. It was the way the world whirled on a mad merry-go-round as soon as my eyes closed. Other friends had talked about being sick drunk but I'd had had no idea what they meant. Who knew that four orange juice drinks could nearly kill you?

"Go away!" she hissed just behind the door. "I never want to see you again."

I said, my thick voice too loud. "It's not your fault. I drank too much."

She opened the door far enough for me to see her nose and one eye cocked sideways above a chain.

"Go away," she said, vehemently. "You'll wake my parents."

"But I… it wasn't my fault. I didn't know." I could still feel the warmth of her body all over mine. I was careful not to breathe on her.

"Well. It certainly wasn't my fault."

"But I… love you." My last futile shot in a lost war.

That stopped her for a second. "Hah!" she said, after a moment, in a slightly less angry voice, the door snapping firmly shut, the dead bolt slamming on my jail cell, the sound of her steps diminishing upstairs.

And that was my first date, at a time in the past when there were dates.

The School Bus No Longer Stops in Front of the House

Evan L. Balkan

My girlfriend left me four days before my uncle's funeral.

"Will you at least come with me to the service?" I asked.

But the deceased wasn't really my uncle—rather, a longtime family friend—and, she reminded me, she was no longer my girlfriend.

It was, unsurprisingly, a somber affair. Worse, I didn't really know anyone. There were some familiar faces, sure, but they were familiar only in the peculiarities that stay lodged in one's memory: a droopy eyelid, a cleaved chin, some wicked palsy or unfortunate birthmark in the shape of New Zealand. I left without saying anything to anyone, my heart in a thousand pieces because she was not there with me.

We could have made fun of the guy with the awful toupee. Then, sitting in a café afterward, we could have upbraided ourselves for being at a funeral and making fun of a guy with an awful toupee. Instead, I came alone and left alone.

I still had my flashers on and the neon orange FUNERAL tag hanging from my rearview mirror when I pulled away from the motorcade, taking a left when everyone else went straight through a red light, respectful drivers waiting out their green. There was a slight delay when the driver behind me stopped, started to follow, decided better of it, and then went on through.

I didn't look back for very long, didn't want to see the faces in that car gaping at me in confusion.

I drove all the way home with my flashers on, still with the FUNERAL tag hanging, passing through a succession of small towns as if I was the president, everyone giving right of way to the lost sheep who'd been separated from the procession and was struggling to make its way back. The blinking lights, the neon orange: they gave me license, and I took hold of it like a possession rightfully mine, something I would not relinquish.

She'd left me, and everyone else was respecting my mourning. I would not give that up so easily.

———————

First, it was bocce. She joined a league. But then she stopped going. It hurt her wrist, she complained. She tried to learn Russian and then when she gave that up, she took up painting. I teased her, sweetly, but she didn't laugh. While she painted, I played video games, hyper-aware of my swerving, jerking body English. In another room, she swerved and jerked, too, paintbrush in hand, a rainbow of droplets spattered across her jeans and t-shirt and face and hair, an enormous canvas the recipient of her angry strokes, each one an exorcism of something deep I never knew, a chipping away of psychic bruises while I blew away swamp monsters or swarthy terrorists or raced through the streets of Monte Carlo in a Bugatti Chiron.

She stayed up late and was grumpy in the morning, and I grew frustrated and angry.

Her expression turned hard, her body sharp.

"You don't understand me," she spat.

"How can I? You're a different person every week."

She smiled—a weary, end-of-the-line smile that said *You're hopeless.* "Every person on Earth is a thousand different people, every hour of every day. Can't you see that?"

I shook my head, out of both genuine confusion and obstinate consternation. I didn't understand it then, hardly understand it now. But I'm working on it. I do understand that her belief in that idea is likely the reason I'm here and she's somewhere else. I imagine this is what war wounded feel like—some essential part of yourself has been ripped out of you. It's like oxygen, a thing you feel more in absence than presence.

I sit in the backyard of my house. It's a sublime day: early October, the sky an eggshell blue. Suggestions of cloud are strung like cotton candy across the horizon. A lone jet trails a stream of white. The maples have started turning. The grass is a deep green, fed by recent rains. I wiggle my toes in the coolness and feel the slither of tears falling down my cheeks. I tell myself that I'm crying from the beauty of it all, the exquisite perfection of an early autumn day. But I know that isn't it. I find myself crying, weeping even, more and more these days. Crying for the flattened fox at the end of the lane. Crying for my mother, who lives alone and who always seems to be in pain but who smiles to cover it up, who always says, "Nothing" and "I'm fine" when I ask her what's wrong. Crying during AARP commercials, stupid movies, Subaru ads.

Crying because I'm crying. Crying when I hear "Dear Prudence." Crying preemptively: for the inevitable day that the smell of her will have dissipated completely from my home, for the day I will not be able to recall her so clearly anymore. I will forget her phone number. The digits will swim in my mind's eye, but they will not line up. They will displace one another, skip spots in line, disperse altogether.

I listen to country music. I hate country music. I imagine living in some godforsaken patch of nowhere—some place in Nebraska or Wyoming, some place achingly beautiful in its insistent, defiant desolation. A place to love for its very hardness. But it was us I used to see there. Now, only me, and I can't imagine anything worse. I used to see its hardscrabble pioneering allure. I see now a man alone, wiping a dish, illuminated by a single dusty bulb above a sink, a shadow, a silhouette, nothingness, a curiosity and caution for some solitary ranging coyote.

⸺ ⋆ ⸺

Out of the corner of my eye, I see the scuttling against the wall as if something is fleeing. I'd opened the closet door and there it went, a wispy mass picking its way along the toe boards: three of her hairs enwrapped in dust. I carry it to the trash, biting my lip. I try to deposit it, but it clings to me. As I shake my hand, it wraps itself tighter around my fingers. I smile at this and then extract the three hairs, putting them on a desk, before letting the dust ball fall easily into the can. I tell myself that it's a joke, that I will keep these hairs and make a doll of it, ha ha. But then I spend the next six hours scouring every centimeter of the house for more hair. When

I'm done—the corner behind the headboard was a goldmine—I've accumulated a fist sized sponge of her hair, which I keep on top of the desk. It's a joke, I tell himself. Just a joke. But it's a joke I will not tell anyone else.

I sleep. But it isn't really sleep. Rather, a fitful battle against memory and ghost.

In the morning, bleary, I grab my funeral tag and drive to my mother's with the flashers on. Everyone gives me the right of way.

I bring her an envelope of legal documents: condo association rules and regs for the beach house, tax forms for renting it out. I've promised to head down there, clean it up, make sure everything's in order after the rental season. But I haven't gone. We were supposed to have gone together. Her and me. And now she's gone. I can't bring myself to go.

"I promise, Ma," I say. "I'm just really busy now."

"With what?" she asks, but I don't answer. I'm half out the door, my mother's handicapped tag in my hands.

I have no food at home, at least nothing I would eat. Instead, it's cans of this and boxes of that, but nothing in the fridge. I haven't eaten much since she's been gone. I go to the grocery store, the old one out in the dying part of town, where no one goes after dark. We used to shop together at the chichi place near the refurbished docks, the one that drove out most of the grocery stores everyone's parents and grandparents went to. I can't go there anymore. Not alone.

I park in the handicapped spot and hang my mother's tag. From there to the door, I drag my left foot behind me and curl three fingers on my left hand. But by the time I leave the store, I've forgotten about it altogether and only remember after I've walked by my car four times because I haven't remembered where I parked. It was just to see, I tell himself. I wasn't trying to gain favor.

I return the tag to my mom—slip it under the door—and hurry home, ashamed of myself.

I set the groceries on the counter.

I go to throw away the funeral tag, but it slips from my hand and quavers its way in a series of perfect arcs until settling under the fridge. I take to the floor and spot a stray Cheerio next to the tag. It's pocked and covered in gray fur. Was it hers, the Cheerio? Did it roll off the counter as she ran through her morning, radio on, standing near the sink, eating cereal, hair up in a sloppy bun, and fuzzy pink socks in which she used to slide from room to room?

I place it in the butter slot in the fridge. The cold will keep it preserved.

The birds. They won't shut up. I slam shut the windows, cover my ears.

We were walking in the woods—it was our woods, and we visited in different seasons: summer, when we'd gone farther than we'd planned and lingered too long and the crowning trees blocked out the fading daylight and we stumbled over rocks and roots but came across glowing moss and diamonds of light in spider webs and raindrops. It was a kind of impossible fantasy. Even without the moss, those woods were themselves a species of magic, a large deep tract somehow spared from dense civilization crowding every side.

Winter—it had snowed during the day but the night was still and not at all cold, and we ran through the woods and hid from each other and found each other and the going was easy because there was a full moon, enough light to read by. We chased, we laughed. We were in love.

We came back in spring, listening to the birds, and when we returned home, she retrieved two glasses and a bottle of wine and dragged the Adirondack chairs to the lip of the lawn.

"God," she marveled. "How is it that one tiny creature can give the world such a beautiful gift?"

"What do you mean?"

"The birds. I mean, it's just, so, beautiful."

I sniggered. "They're not doing it for our pleasure. When birds sing, it's a warning. They're protecting the nest."

I'd heard something like that before, though I wondered then if that was true. Didn't they sing to attract mates as well? And couldn't a bird have a beautiful mating song and also a mean squawk for defense? In any case, I was certain there was at least some sliver of truth to it. I was sure these birds weren't just happy creatures singing for our benefit. The world just didn't work that way.

"What do you think? Only crows and blue jays are angry? Songbirds don't care about their young?" I asked.

She didn't say anything. Then she lifted herself off her chair and walked inside. The door shut behind her, first with a bang and then with a series of dying taps. The fading sunlight caught the lip of her wine glass. Rainbows swum and swirled in the clinging droplets, a strand of her saliva thickening it, combining all the elements of the universe I could ever want or need—sun, earth, liquid, her—before it slid along the inside of the glass and disappeared into dark purple depths. The sun left the glass, then the leaves, then the near side of the Earth altogether, and I sat in the gathering darkness and waited.

But she didn't return.

Eventually, something from one of the grocery bags drips off the counter. But still I sit on the couch, immovable.

Putting my hand on her stomach. That's what I can't forget. The warmth. The initial tensing of the skin to my touch, followed by the loosening. The trust. Then her hand on top of mine, without speaking. Below our hands, deep inside her, one day a new life. One we would have created.

We tried, once. We rolled the dice, ready. The school bus had just made its stop in front of the house, the little neighbor boy sprinting to the bifold door, a glove falling into the street, where it would be left behind, run over, dimpled with pebble and grime.

"So convenient," she cooed. "Our little shaver will only have to run across the lawn to catch the bus." And then we were in the bedroom, even before the growl of the bus's engine had fully trailed off.

She looked up at me. "I can't read your expression," she said.

"Huh?"

"On your face. You look… I don't know what it is. I've never seen you look that way."

I stopped. "What way?"

"You look… guilty. You look like a boy who's been caught stealing."

I felt myself softening inside her.

She was on her elbows now, talking as if we were doing a crossword puzzle. "You look like you're going to cry or explode or something."

I lay back and stared at the ceiling, pulling the covers up to my neck.

I knew what it was. It was Amazement. Gratitude. Wonder. I was inside her. It was like some kind of miracle, to enter another human being. I supposed a woman could say the same thing, or the obverse. That she knows what it feels like to have someone inside her. But it seemed a pale comparison. I was the one with the winning proposition, being a man, the gifts bestowed upon me by nature and biological logistics. I was the one who, when she asked me to explain my expression, was making memories not for selfish future retrieval but because these memories: the feel of her rib cage as she inhaled, the sight of the dimples at the edges of her spine—these I was committing to memory so that if nothing else in this life, I had that, and she was offering it up to me and I was flushed and alive with love and gratitude for it... this is why I looked like a dope, or whatever I looked like that she couldn't describe. I was happy. Pure happiness. That is what the look was.

But I couldn't explain myself and when she eventually got out of bed and put on her clothes, still I couldn't say anything. Because, yes, I had an evolutionary endpoint hanging from my body—lucky me—but the thousands of years of biology that led the universe to the edges of myself, were, I was realizing, subsumed entirely by one salient fact: Men also have hearts. And hearts can be shattered.

<hr />

She'd abandoned a decent lot of her clothes. I'd called, texted, emailed: "You coming over to get your clothes?" She never responded. She already had a new boyfriend, I assumed. She may have had a new boyfriend even while she was still with me. Losing some clothes was, apparently, a small price to pay for extricating herself wholesale. I imagine her new boyfriend saying: "Forget that stuff. We'll go shopping and buy new clothes." I imagine her smiling at this, kissing him lightly on the lips. I remember when clothes, and food, and air seemed superfluous—nothing was necessary, not one single thing, when you were in love. Nothing, that is, apart from love.

I buy a wig. I put on one of her blouses. It's tight across the middle and I let out a few stitches. I pad the area at the breast. I put on some old jeans, smear my face with makeup after shaving with a straight razor.

I pick my spots carefully—coffee shops in the city's hipster enclaves, radical bookstores near the art college. A place named Alexandra's, after a Russian Communist revolutionary, where girls with severe haircuts and black horn-rimmed glasses and a penchant for plaid and safety pins glower over enormous coffee mugs and tasteless pastries. Sugar, apparently, is a bourgeoisie affectation. I enter the women's bathroom, but it's the women's bathroom only by default. There are two bathrooms, both labeled "gender neutral," but old habits and the faint remnants of "Men" and "Women" stenciled above each lintel still shadow the hasty paint job, which means one of them is, by default, for women, and the other for men.

The women in the bathroom do not treat me with alarm or even curiosity, but rather with nods of solidarity. I make no show of hiding the fact that I'm standing above a toilet, the stall door open. It's as if they can tell that I'm not there to try to catch a glimpse of someone. And they're right: I'm in there to relieve myself, after all—nothing more.

And when I'm done, I leave, feeling absolutely no sense of accomplishment or enlightenment at all.

Back at home, it hits me as I walk through my front door: it sprints to my brain at full force. I snap up a pencil from the wire holder on the desk. I can picture pencils clamped between her teeth so vividly that I expect them to still be wet with her saliva. But they're not. No teeth marks, either. I pick up another and then another. Each is missing its eraser—had she swallowed them? —and each smells of lead and hollow metal cups. But no indentations. I feel a bubbling rage inside me, melting quickly into despair. I want those teeth marks, need them. For proof. Proof that she'd lived here, had shared her life with me, had reverted to some kind of childishness when she put pencils between her teeth and bit down.

But maybe I'd imagined it. Maybe I'd imagined everything.

I catch sight of myself in the mirror. A homely woman with a jutting Adam's apple stares back at me. I change my clothes and toss the wig in the garbage. I wipe away the makeup, but it smudges, caked like clown paint. So I get into the shower, where the spray bats at the back of my hanging head. I reach for the shower gel and there, tucked behind extraneous bottles of various shampoos and conditioners, her apple blossom shampoo. I inhale, as if the very essence of her is trapped inside. Again, deeply, and again, again until it smells like nothing anymore. I close it up, put it back. I will not allow any more of it, of her, to escape. I will save it until it molders.

We'd stumbled upon an old apple orchard, once, I can't recall where. Derelict, with apples already mush on the ground, worm-eaten and browned by sun and rain. But many still clung to branches and offered themselves like little miracles: splinters of yellow and red streaking rounded edges from stem to puckered bottom.

Even though it was clear that this orchard hadn't been tended, it felt like trespassing and at any moment there would materialize someone with a shotgun pointed at our chests. But that made it more exciting. Isn't that the very essence of love? Of paradise? And what is paradise anyway, but a place from which we can at any moment, for any transgression, be expelled?

So we picked our way quietly, marveling, and while I stood watch at the crest of a hill with a view of a valley beneath where I imagined a cabin hidden in the woods, a place sheltering a jealous or paranoid owner, she collected a dozen pristine apples and loaded up the hem of her dress. When I turned around and saw her like that, white sundress loaded with fruit, a smile as wide as the moon across her face, the incredible innocence of it—she may as well have been a six year-old—I couldn't breathe or swallow. Where in the western world do women collect fruit in the hems of their dresses anymore?

It is this image: the fruit of the vine, the fruit of her, that wakes me at night, gasping, and all I can do is reach out, grab hold of something that isn't there. Awake, I think about: A harbor. We'd visited one once, together, some late fall day full of crisp sunshine that turned cold the moment the sun started to sink, a cruel reminder to savor and hold on, breathe deep the clang of boats, metal on metal, the wheeling gulls, faint faraway laughter, the feeling that you were in on something grand and yet so tiny, compressed into a square of Earth where she and I were together, fingers interlaced, steps synchronized.

How can the absence of a thing feel more a presence than even the presence of it ever did?

There is work to be done still.

———

I slip into my best suit and head to a cemetery to catch the funeral service of a Mr. Grady Templeton: world traveler, Francophile, and employee of C.S. Burton & Assoc. This, according to the obit that appeared in the Post-Gazette. I did not pick up a new funeral tag. I will no longer engage in that childishness. I am growing. I have, for example, considered and then rejected donning blackface and trying to gain entry to places I never otherwise go. Will probably look like I have a disease, I imagine. Instead, I go to the cemetery straight, the singular man I am.

When the coffin has been lowered and the mourners have gone away, I remain, watching three Latino men shovel on the dirt. I stay because of the unspoken mandate she had left me, some unfinished project which I have, so far, failed miserably.

Soon, a paunchy middle-aged man sidles up, reeking of cucumbers, the pickled smell of an alcoholic wafting from every pore. The man breathes out an ammoniac aroma with a long exhalation of surprise or disgust or wonder.

"So, how'd you know Ol' Grady?" he asks.

"We used to work together. Years ago."

"At Burton?"

"That's right. At Burton. He was good."

The man lets out a guffaw. "Yeah, right. If that was true, after thirty years he would have risen beyond middle management. Real piece of work… with the way that man drank, no wonder they didn't have him cremated. Sonofabitch would have burned for three weeks."

"I slept with his wife."

The man's face lights up with surprise and delight. "Wonderful! Which one?"

"The first one."

"Dolores?"

I nod.

The man slaps me on the shoulder in congratulation or pity or both. "You're a braver man than I am. Speak no ill of the dead and all, but, geez… what was she? Two-seventy-five? Two eighty?"

I feel an obligation to defend this Delores, this woman who deserves respect, this woman I do not know and never did, another ghost, another figment. "She was wonderful, if you want to know the truth."

"I'm not sure I do."

The man totters away, whistling, laughing to himself.

"Everyone deserves to be respected," I yell after the man. "Everyone. And every different person inside everyone."

The man waves a dismissive hand and laughs, picking his way unsteadily across the rows of granite.

<hr>

The school bus route has changed. It no longer stops in the neighborhood. There are no more kids left. The neighbors have moved, and in any case, the kid who used to ride the bus is no longer in elementary school.

I hear its absence, every morning at 8:31, its ghostly grinding of brakes, its rumbling approach, its exhaust-filled departure. All this I see, hear, smell, more acutely now that we are no longer.

She'd told me that every person, every person on Earth, is a thousand different people.

Except that I wasn't. I am still, and forever will be, one person. And the thousand people within me, living, loving, dying, reincarnating, every hour, every day, still only total up to one.

And that, for better or worse, is all I'll ever be.

Drought Summer
John Guzlowski

See my little girl, Lillian?
She can read a book

make change for a twenty
tell you what star is what

She doesn't need
School or love or dolls.

She knows winter is hard
And beds are soft

pumpkins
grow on vines.

She knows
what's useless:

the soft spade
the easy turn.

Maybe in Mississippi
somewhere

the soil is wet and sweet
ready for asparagus

or juicy fruit
but not here.

Here the ground is clay
more clay than dirt.

Here, if you see a dog,
you know he's leaving.

Patricide
Paula Rudnick

This is how I'd kill my father:

Take him out for yogurt
at the mall near the dementia place,
order him a chocolate cone,
slide pills into the swirls.
He'd want to share, too big for one,
but I'd just say, eat what you can,
then watch him take another bite,
the way he puts one foot before the other
without knowing where he's going.

Is this my life now? he asks sadly
when we drop him in the room
with the chair he doesn't sit in
and tv he doesn't watch.
He doesn't understand
how his clothes got in the closet
or why the rest of us can leave
when they take him down to dinner.
He's mad that the attendants make him
brush his teeth and change his pants,
and he can't shave inside the dining room at lunch.
Of course you can't, my mother says.
She talks to him like he's still real.

I was hoping for a blood clot
when they called to say he fell,
a bubble to his brain to take him out,
but he was fine.
His legs weep fluid, drenching pants and socks,
the fleece-lined scuffs he slides around in—
grizzled phantom in a terry robe.

Eat your yogurt, I would tell him
if I didn't lose my nerve,
resigned to soldier on like he is,
one foot past the other,
till the white flag's hoisted
and it's safe to carry off our dead.

In the Lemon Orchard

Dallas Woodburn

That summer, Rae's round face smiled from MISSING posters throughout the city. I taped the posters to lampposts and slipped them under windshield wipers and stuffed them into mailboxes. If I give her photograph to every single person in Ventura, then she will come home, and everything will be okay.

But Rae stayed missing.

Authorities combed the lemon orchard but found nothing. Not a charm from her bracelet. Not a pink shoelace. Not a single strand of her dark hair.

A suspect was never named.

A funeral was never held.

That winter, Rae's family moved away. I never set foot in the orchard again.

June in Ventura is a gloomy month. The fog creeps in from the ocean and stretches its fingers inland, settling in the creases of the hills, the spaces between office buildings, the narrow yards of houses. Cars maneuver slowly down Foothill Road, their headlights on even in the middle of the afternoon. The fog makes seeing difficult. It seeps down Main Street, covering the shops and restaurants so only the heads of the palm trees and the arching buttresses of the movie theater stretch above it, peering over the fog like tall people peer over a crowd. The fog sinks down over the lemon orchards like a thick blanket, catching in the branches of trees and wrapping the small, unripened lemons in fists of dew.

The air is chilly and damp. Sweater weather. In the fog, even the most familiar streets seem cloaked in secrets. The entire town feels quiet, under siege.

On summer mornings, Rae and I would escape into the fog after breakfast and race down the block, across El Dorado Street, and into the lemon orchard. Our favorite tree was an old, gnarled beauty seven rows up, far enough from El Dorado that traffic noise didn't reach us. The lemon orchard was our place, our Shell and Rae Hideaway, and on foggy days, its mystery was amplified, its solitude more pronounced. On foggy days, anything could happen.

Rae disappeared on a foggy day.

When my parents bought this house, it was a new house in a new housing development. I was just over a year old. I don't remember living anywhere else, don't remember the fresh-paint, new-carpet smell of the big empty rooms. I've seen pictures, snapped on a disposable camera, of the house when it was brand new—vulnerable flower beds and the mulberry tree just a sapling, braced with wooden stakes. I can't remember the tree as anything less than magnificent, its leafy branches stretching toward the sky, perfect for climbing.

Rae's family moved in across the street when I was three. One of my earliest memories is sitting in a little red wagon with Rae, being pulled along the sidewalk by Rae's older brother, Jonathan. Rae had shiny dark hair and a moon-shaped birthmark on her right knee. She wore a silver charm bracelet and bright pink tennis shoes. She liked holding my hand, and her hands were always cool and dry. Even as we grew older, even as we stopped holding our parents' hands to cross the street, Rae would still grab mine when she was excited. As if she were trying to transfer the emotion between our palms.

As kids, we shared every shivery detail of our lives. Rae's distrust of the ice-cream man. My dream of drowning. Rae's love of lime-green Skittles. My fear of snails. We were born a year and a month apart, and I often daydreamed that Rae was my sister, and that I had been given to my parents because Rae's family already had Jonathan and Rae, and my parents didn't have anyone. As a kid, my hair sprang up in unruly blonde curls, and my compact frame was the opposite of Rae's willowy height. But we had the same sun-freckled shoulders, and I liked to imagine the same blood flowed through our veins.

Until the foggy June I turned fourteen, and suddenly Rae didn't feel like a sister anymore. I noticed inklings of new feelings, strange and awkward. I tried to ignore them. I tried to push them away. But my feelings only expanded—like an overripe lemon, skin stretched taught with pulp and juice, ready to drop from the tree.

<hr>

I began running track shortly after Rae's family moved away. I run the mile and the two-mile. I have a habit of vomiting after races. Coach says I push myself too hard.

My dad attends all my track meets. He's a firm believer in positive reinforcement. His own parents never attended a single one of his boyhood tennis matches or football games.

My mom defends Grandma and Grandpa. "They had five kids to worry about. We only have Michelle."

Still, there are a lot of track meets, and my dad hasn't missed a single one. He always settles himself in the top row of the rickety wooden bleachers, wearing his green windbreaker and bright yellow baseball cap, and gives me a thumb's up as I nervously jog to the starting line. There's something fierce and protective in my dad's devotion to my track meets, as if he is trying to ward off ever-lurking danger, control what's uncontrollable. Driving home after the meets, he puts on his Best of James Taylor CD. Sometimes I feel like talking about the race, and my dad turns the volume down. Other times I gaze out the window, silent and spent, and the only voice in the car is James' crooning.

"When I was Michelle's age," my dad once said at the dinner table, "I remember, I'd always glance at the stands, hoping to see my parents. It would have been great to see them there. To know they were proud of me."

"Of course, they were proud of you," my mom said. "It was a different time then. People didn't say 'I love you.' They didn't need to. You just knew."

<hr>

When Rae's family moved away, I sobbed in the bathroom, my cheek pressed against the cool tile. My mom came in with freshly laundered towels and found me.

"Honey, oh baby," she said, coaxing me off the floor and onto my bed, stroking my hair.

"I loved her," I sobbed. "I loved her so much."

"I know you did."

"No, I mean I loved her, Mom. I still am in love with her."

Mom smoothed my hair away from my forehead. "Oh, honey. You don't know what love is. This is called grieving."

"She was my soulmate," I said.

"Dr. Stevenson says it's normal for you to feel this way." Mom reached over and plucked a tissue from the box on the nightstand. "Shelly, listen to me. It's going to be okay," she said. "You're a strong girl. You're going to be okay. Someday this will all feel like a long time ago."

***

That June day, the day Rae disappeared, the day everything changed, I ran upstairs to my bathroom and vomited into the toilet. I leaned against the sink, swishing mouthwash around and around my teeth. It stung my gums. I kept swishing. Finally, I spat it out. I kept spitting. Fiercely. Rhythmically. My eyes squeezed shut, as if in prayer.

***

My lips had felt chapped when I finally pushed Jonathan away. I wiped my mouth with the back of my hand and pulled my shirt back down over my bra. Jonathan looked at the ground. He asked if I was okay, then sighed.

"I think it'll be best if this is our secret," he said.

I nodded. My legs felt hollow.

"Rae's not in my room," I told him. "I was being honest."

"I'm sure she's at my house then," Jonathan said. "I probably just missed her somehow."

As we left the orchard, the fog was clearing. I searched for the moon, but it was a new moon, only a tiny sliver of light in the darkness.

———————————

I'd led Jonathan through the orchard, exhilarated anger fizzing inside me, picturing the shock that would fill Rae's face upon seeing her brother in our hideaway. I wanted to see hurt in Rae's eyes. I wanted to show Rae that it didn't matter, none of it—all our whispered confessions, our jokes, our promises—it was all just childhood stuff. Silly games. Pretending.

I didn't know I was going to kiss Jonathan until we reached the old gnarled lemon tree and found it empty. Unease clenched my belly, but I told myself Rae was nearby. The next tree over. Watching.

"It's so dark here," I said. And it was. Tree shadows loomed with outstretched arms.

"Is this the one?" Jonathan asked, nudging his foot against the lemon tree.

"Yep. This is our hideout."

"Rae?" Jonathan called. "Rae!"

"Rae!" I yelled.

Somewhere in the distance, an owl hooted.

I stepped closer to Jonathan. "It's spooky in here," I said, hugging my arms.

Jonathan looked down at me, and something shifted in his expression. "You scared?" he said, putting an arm around me. His arm was heavy, and his arm-hair prickled my bare back.

I nodded and bit my lip. I was scared, suddenly. Rae and I never ventured into the orchard after dark. Everything felt heightened. The rustling of the leaves, the shadowed trunks of the trees were like something out of a fever-dream.

"Don't be scared," Jonathan said, tightening his arm around me. There was something in his voice that I had never heard there before. I knew what was going to happen and I imagined Rae was hiding nearby, watching. Defiantly, I tilted my face up to Jonathan's.

It was not what I expected. It was not sweet or gentle. His beard was rough against my cheek. He pressed me against the tree, and I felt fear expand until it filled me completely.

"What about Rae?" I said. "We should find Rae."

Jonathan grinned. "You and I both know why you brought me here, and it wasn't to find Rae. She's upstairs in your room right now." He leaned closer. He smelled of sweat and cigarettes. "I could always tell you had a thing for me."

On foggy days, anything could happen.

It was Rae I thought about as he held me to him, his hands pulling at my hair. I thought of Rae and I felt angry and panicky, like the order of the world had fallen away. I kept my eyes closed. His mouth tasted like the ocean, bitter and acrid.

When I'd heard the knocking, I hadn't wanted to answer the door. I thought it was Rae, wanting to apologize, to explain, to talk. I knew I couldn't handle seeing Rae. Not for a while.

But the knocking persisted, so I undid the latch and yanked the door open. Rae's brother Jonathan stood on the front porch. Behind him, the sun sank blearily through the fog. Jonathan was sixteen, with Rae's dark hair but a thicker build and curling, sarcastic lips. He was growing a beard and it shadowed his jowls in patches.

"Rae's supposed to come home. It's time for dinner," he said.

"She's not here."

"She's not?"

I shrugged. "Sorry. I don't know where she is."

"Bullshit, you two are attached at the hip. I know she's hiding in your room or something. It's her night to do the dishes and I'm not letting her push it off on me again."

"We were hanging out earlier, but then I had to leave. You can search my room if you want. She's not there."

"Well, she hasn't come home," Jonathan said. "It'll be dark soon. You know better than me where she could be."

Rae and I were eight years old when we first ventured into the orchard and claimed the gnarled lemon tree as our hideaway. "I have an idea," Rae had said. "Let's promise never to show this place to anyone. It's our secret." I promised. Rae stole a paring knife from her family's cutlery drawer, and we carved our names into the tree trunk.

"I think I know where she is," I told Jonathan. I hollered to my parents that I was going over to Rae's for dinner, then stepped outside and closed the door behind me. "C'mon, I'll show you."

I had known as soon as Rae pulled away. She wasn't smiling. Shame lurked in her eyes. She untangled her hand from mine and wiped her mouth, the charms on her bracelet clinking softly against each other. Neither of us spoke. My hands shook as I swung myself down from the tree. Leaves littered the ground. I ran.

Rae called after me, tears in her voice: "You're my best friend!"

I kept running.

Rae's lips were chapped. Her tongue tasted of bubblegum toothpaste.

That June day, Rae and I perched side-by-side on a branch of our lemon tree. The fog curled around us. Rae's hair glistened darkly in the shadows. Her bare shoulder leaned against mine, a warm steady weight. Our legs dangled, our thighs touched. The moon-shaped birthmark on Rae's knee winked up at me, as if it knew my secret.

Rae whistled a few notes. "Is that how the song goes?"

"What song?"

"That one we heard on the radio. I can't remember the words."

"I don't know," I said.

Rae whistled the notes again. Her voice sounded loud in the stillness of the orchard. Then, abruptly, she stopped, turning to me with wide eyes.

"Did you hear that?" she whispered.

"What?"

"I swear I just heard a footstep."

"I didn't hear anything."

"Someone's out there," Rae said. She nestled her body closer to mine. Beneath us, the tree branch shifted. A lemon fell and thumped softly on the ground.

"There," Rae said. "What was that?"

I laughed. "It was a lemon. You're such a dork."

"I think someone's out there." Rae reached for my hand.

The dark leaves whispered to each other. The fog pressed close.

I met Rae's eyes. Then I leaned in, lips parted, knowing that nothing would ever be the same.

(you, already else
where)

Mary Silwance

this is what I do now:
    (you, already else

                where)
    text you back from another room
    remind you to wear the backpack on both shoulders
    to protect your spine
    listen poker-faced to your music even as it cringes me
    not know your every friend's name
    wait for you to want a hug
    help decide if the silver dangling or studs
    match the maroon Converse
        I feel the weight of this (even
        as I am almost certain of the
        someday unweight of it)

take the banana skin offhanded me

                a relic

from
when we were not separate, not really
when you offered me everything:

    snot smears across the shirt belly
    spent gum in my palm
    farts on my lap
    playground drama misted
    in my cupped ear
    stubbed toe to kiss
    thirteen part handshake

the banana skin: intact with all that

At Last and Too Soon
Corrie Haldane

My jellyfish paperweight moved again today.

Last night when I went to bed, it sat in its customary spot on my desk, next to the Disney mug I use to hold pens, highlighters, and assorted dried out markers. This morning when I woke up, I discovered it on the bathroom counter beside the toothpaste.

Yesterday I found it in my purse. The day before that, the refrigerator. Once I found it tucked into my left running shoe. Over and over, I return it to its rightful place, hoping it will finally stay put, knowing that it probably won't.

I snatch it up, braced for the jolt of ice-cold glass in my hand. "Maybe I'll just throw it off the balcony this time," I say.

I hope he is listening even though he can't possibly be listening. It doesn't matter; I'm bluffing anyway.

I return the paperweight to its home on my desk, run a finger along the newly warmed glass. "Oh, Nick," I whisper. "What do you want?"

But I already know.

"Jellyfish can live forever, you know."

That was the first thing Nick ever said to me. We were in the fourth grade.

The other boys and girls didn't have much to do with Nick. He was the weird new kid who lived with his aunt because he didn't have any parents. The other boys and girls didn't have much to do with me either, though, so I didn't care what they thought.

"I don't believe you," I said. "Nothing lives forever."

"Some things can," he assured me. "And one day, people will too. You'll see."

Many years later, he gave me the paperweight as a birthday gift. My breath caught in my throat when I opened the plain white box and peeled back layers of tissue paper to reveal a perfectly preserved jellyfish suspended in glass.

"Jellyfish live forever," I said.

"Actually, it's only a certain species of jellyfish," Nick corrected. "And even then, they're still vulnerable to predators, they can still die by violence. They're only immortal if they're left alone."

I wondered if he was thinking about the car accident that robbed him of his parents when he was just a little boy. My heart ached for him.

"I love it." I leaned in to give him a hug. He pulled me close and held me for a moment, but all too soon, he pulled back. Turned away. Just like always.

Nick, like the jellyfish, felt safer when left alone.

I'm three months older than Nick. Or I was. I'm not sure how that works anymore, now that he's gone. Despite that, for our entire twenty-year friendship, it's always been me who chased after him, like a little sister desperate not to be left behind by the big brother who had better things to do with his time.

In high school, I joined the school paper and tried out for the track team. He rushed through all his classes as though he couldn't wait to get home to his computer and his solitude. He avoided all extracurricular activities until Computer Club in senior year, and that was just to pad his college applications.

Nobody would have called me popular, but I managed to make a few friends. Nick only had me, and I never knew for sure whether he'd even notice if I stopped being there. Not that I'd ever abandon him.

We spent many nights on the phone, often talking until way past midnight. We hung out face to face too, but our best conversations happened at a distance, through the wires. Maybe because it felt safer when we couldn't see each other. Safer to be our real selves, talk about things that truly mattered.

Nick often spoke about things that sounded more like science fiction to me. "Cryonics, Tara. That's what I'm going to study when I finally get out of this stupid town," he told me. "It's basically putting your body into deep freeze until scientists discover how to reverse aging and cure all the big diseases."

"Then what?" I asked. "They just… thaw you out again on some distant day, when they finally figure all that out?"

"Yeah, pretty much."

I imagined falling into a long, cold sleep. Waking to a different world, one where everyone I loved was long gone. "But why?"

"Some people believe there's a heaven waiting for us after we die," he said. "That's just a fantasy, a fairy tale. Science can make heaven a reality, right here on Earth."

Sometimes I read Nick my poems. Never the ones full of heartache and longing, though. Nick was my best friend; he called me his soul sister. I could never risk losing that by sharing verse that exposed my deeper feelings.

He always listened and he often gave thoughtful critiques of my work. Even though Nick was fluent in metaphor and imagery, he preferred to speak computer languages and mathematics instead.

"There's more than one way to write a poem, Tara," he told me. "Coding is poetic, too."

"Uh huh," I said with obvious sarcasm. "Sure it is."

"Listen," he said. "Did you know that scientists think they'll be able to basically upload your brain onto a computer just a few short years from now? You don't need a body to be you—it's your memories, your likes and dislikes… that's what makes up what you really are. You don't think that's beautiful? In a virtual world, you can be anywhere and everywhere all the time. Forever."

"I just want to write poems," I said. "Maybe people will still read my words years after I'm gone and that's how I'll live forever."

"That's not living," Nick scoffed.

"But your way—inside a computer—that is?"

"It's better than nothing," he said. I could tell he believed that, too.

I return to the bathroom, halfway expecting to find the paperweight on the counter again, but everything is as it should be. I take a long shower and even though the water's as hot as I can stand, I can't seem to get warm.

After my shower, I wrap up in my thick terry bathrobe and return to my desk. My computer is on now. It wasn't before. It's open to my emails and I watch, dumbfounded, as the little arrow crawls across the screen and hovers on the compose button and then a blank email pops up. The cursor blinks at me from the To box.

I sit down, drop my fingers to the keys, and start to type.

"This is crazy," I mutter, several paragraphs in. I delete the email, unsent.

I return to my bedroom to dress and find a tattered copy of The Oracle, the campus lit mag from my college days, propped up on my pillow. It's open to a poem I wrote called "Swallowing the Doctor."

I had written a whole series of poems about immortality back then. I only ever sent one of them to Nick but he didn't acknowledge it when he finally emailed me back. Shamed, I kept the rest of the series to myself, even when The Oracle accepted that one for publication.

By university, Nick and I had replaced our phone calls with emails. Mine were long and rambling, littered with snippets of poetry that I'd written or read, descriptions of my professors, and gossip about my friends.

Nick's emails were brief. Mostly just links to journal articles about biological engineering and nanotechnology, accompanied by short paragraphs more about science than him. I read every word, even though I barely understood most of the concepts. In my replies, I'd slip in details I'd gleaned, still vying for his approval. His admiration. His love.

The last email Nick ever sent me was on my twenty-ninth birthday. I need to see you. Please come?

I hadn't heard a from him in months; he hadn't even bothered to reply to the weepy, drunken voicemail I'd left him after Mark and I broke up. Suddenly, out of the blue, he was demanding an audience and he hadn't even bothered to wish me a happy birthday. I almost deleted it without answering.

But it was Nick. I could never stay mad at him, even when I wanted to. Even if he deserved it.

I'll be there Saturday, I replied.

I suppose a part of me had always believed that Nick actually would discover the secret to immortality, so the fragile, emaciated Nick that let me into his apartment came as a complete shock.

"Cancer," he said by way of greeting. "It's pretty much all through me now."

He gestured toward the sofa. "Sit."

I watched as he carefully lowered himself into the chair across from me. "Are you being treated? Chemo?"

"Been there, done that, got the tee shirt," he replied.

"What about other options?"

"There are no other options. I'm dying, Tara, and I need you to do something for me."

Nick spoke. I shook my head. I wiped my eyes. He spoke some more.

"No. I'm sorry, Nick. I can't..."

"Dr. Singlar is expecting your call," he said. He held out a business card. I didn't take it.

Nick pinned me in place with the weight of his gaze. "I thought I'd have more time," he said. "I was supposed to have forever. And now..."

"I'm sorry," I repeated. "Call me if there is anything else I can do."

Nick never called. He died less than a week after my visit.

The jellyfish moved for the first time three months later, on his birthday—the first one he wouldn't be around to celebrate. I found the paperweight on the passenger seat of my car.

I stuffed it into my coat pocket and put it back where it belonged when I got home. Then I pushed the memory from my mind, content to pretend that absolutely nothing had happened.

Until it moved again.

The sudden appearance of the old magazine shakes me more than I'd like to admit. That night, I lie awake in bed for hours, tossing and turning, wondering if I'm actually alone. I don't remember falling asleep, but morning sunlight now spills through my bedroom window, so I must have.

I rise and take a careful inventory of my bedroom, expecting to find the paperweight underneath my pillow, or maybe buried in my sock drawer. It's in none of these places, though. I expand my search to the rest of my apartment, and with a surprising mixture of disappointment and relief, I discover it on my desk, right where I'd left it the day before.

I let out a shaky laugh but before I can scold myself for being foolish, I notice the business card Nick had tried to give to me is tucked underneath the glass.

Dr. Singlar, Reproductive Endocrinologist.

With trembling fingers, I pick it up. When I turn it over, I immediately recognize Nick's handwriting. He'd scribbled a quote from "The Summer Day" by Mary Oliver, one of my favorite poets.

Tell me, what else should I have done?

Doesn't everything die at last, and too soon?

I recite the next lines from memory, tears rolling down my cheek. "Tell me, what is it you plan to do with your one wild and precious life?"

I pick up the phone and dial the number on the front of the card.

Seven months later, I have a notebook bursting with new work and a belly bursting with new life.

It only took one round of artificial insemination for me to conceive. I lay on an exam table, feet in stirrups and legs spread wide, while the doctor inserted Nick's healthy sperm, collected and frozen before he'd begun cancer treatments. I'd always hoped that one day, Nick and I might consummate our relationship, but I'd never imagined it would be like this.

Even though it was too soon to be sure, I knew less than a week later that the procedure had been successful because the paperweight disappeared for good.

From within my womb, there is a flutter and a shift. The baby I affectionately refer to as The Jellyfish is restless. Soon she will breathe air, suck milk, shake her tiny fists at the unforgiving universe. But for now, she still dreams drowsily, safe inside of me.

Two Birds

Rosaleen Bertolino

On a summer evening, alone in her bedroom, lying on her hospital bed, Alice studied the streak of gold eye shadow on her wrist. Glittering and rich as the eye of a peacock feather. On her other wrist, the purple looked disappointingly like a bruise. Like many things, she thought, you didn't know how they would turn out until you tried them. This was why you needed to do things while you had the chance. Not always think them over as her parents insisted.

Alice, nineteen, was allowed to try very little. She had cerebral palsy, her body a cage of spasms and seizures, a cage she looked out of, and that people peered into, and because of this cage, it seemed to Alice that no one really knew her.

Her mother, for instance, who bought books about people who overcame their disabilities and went on to do noble things—Stephen Hawking, Helen Keller, that guy in My Left Foot. Her mother wanted Alice to become a saint. Her father, on the other hand, hoped for Alice to remain a little girl, forever. But what Alice wanted was a boyfriend.

Recently, alone in her bed, where she spent altogether too much of her time, Alice had discovered that by rolling over and pressing her pelvis against one or the other of her hands, she could give herself a great deal of pleasure. A great, great deal. She flew into the pleasure and soared out of her body, a small bright bird. Up near the ceiling, she looked down on herself, at the smooth rosy skin, the thick shiny hair, the breasts as full and round as anyone could want.

She imagined a man touching her and the pleasure increased. Lately, even the cool professional attentions of her doctor (the light touch of his fingers on her chin, her ears) had begun to have electrical effects, producing rivulets that sparked along her skin.

She found ways to prolong the appointments after Dr. Engel listened to her heart and lungs, after he checked her ankles and joints for swelling.

"What if… I can't… swallow?" she asked him.

"It's not progressive," Dr. Engel said. But he peered in her mouth to reassure her, and gently manipulated her throat. His hazel eyes so kind. His smile grazed her, she grew warm, tingles ran from her throat and all the way down. And back home, she pressed against her hand.

Alice's health aide was Tama, a born-again Christian from Samoa who talked nonstop. Tama went on and on about Jesus the way the girls in high school had bragged about their boyfriends. God was "awesome" and Tama had been unhappy before she had "found Him." Tama was always inviting Alice to her church, telling Alice that Brother Ford was a miracle worker, but that meant nothing to Alice, who'd never been to any church at all.

One day Tama mentioned that her nephew Tao had come to live with her because he needed to leave Los Angeles in a hurry. He'd done something, something so bad that Tama wouldn't tell Alice what it was. "He needs Jesus," was all Tama would say. That evening, Alice, already partly in love with Tao because of his mysterious wickedness, told her parents that she wanted to go to Tama's church.

"If you're interested in exploring your spiritual side," said her mother, "I expect we can find a church closer to home. I believe Tama's church is Fundamentalist."

"I want… to go!" said Alice.

Alice's parents were the opposite of religious. Both well into their forties when Alice was born; a "wonderful surprise," her mother told her. Alice's father, wiry and stooped, was an economics professor who believed in flow charts. Her placid, bossy mother believed in doctors, psychotherapy, and the power of positive thinking. Whenever the two of them allied against her, Alice didn't stand a chance.

"Religion is a crutch," her father said.

"Of course, we know Tama is important to you," said her mother.

Alice felt herself coming to a boil. It wasn't like she was asking to shoot heroin! "You never… let me do… anything."

Silence. Now her father was droning on, saying that religion was an opiate—nothing but an escape from life's difficulties. And why not, Alice thought. She often dreamed of flying; imagined that being drunk or high might feel as reckless and wonderful. She'd never considered church to be in the same category as drugs. Now she had another reason she wanted to go.

Her mother leaned forward over her lentil soup. "I'll go with you," she said.

If she came, Alice's chance to meet Tao was doomed. "Only me," Alice cried out. "Me and Tama."

Her parents frowned.

"Please don't let anyone take advantage of you," her father said. "I'll remind you again, if anything untoward happens, you must tell us immediately."

Untoward? Only her father, the professor, would use a word like that. Her parents were always warning her that she was vulnerable—as if she were still a child, as if she did not have breasts and pubic hair, or sexual desire.

They'd lectured her a million times. If anyone touched her, anyone at all, in a way that was not appropriate, she should not be afraid to tell them immediately. Such persons were bad, very bad, and now Alice wanted very badly to meet such a person.

"You'll be bored," her mother was saying. "You'll have to sit there and not ask questions. Watch what Tama does and do the same."

Alice beamed, knowing her mother had given in.

———

Sunday morning, Alice insisted on wearing the gold eyeshadow and being dressed in a tight pink top and a fluffy white skirt. On her soft feet, gold sandals that had never touched the ground. She wanted her long hair left unbraided. Her mother, even though she did not believe in God, fussed that she did not look appropriate for church.

"They all dress like this," Alice said, a lie that turned out to be true.

As Tama maneuvered Alice's wheelchair into the van, Tao stood off to one side. Like Tama, he was large and bulky with smooth ash-brown skin. His sturdy face had the sullen air of a captive. He said nothing to Alice or her parents when introduced, just ducked his head and shoved his hands deeper into the pockets of his oversized jeans, tapping his big feet in their white sneakers. He was dressed like a tough boy, the too-large pants so loose on his hips that his underwear showed.

While Tama drove, going on about Jesus and the beautiful summer day, Tao sat silently in the back of the van. Alice wondered whether he thought she was pretty. Her hair was her best feature, thick, shiny, halfway down her back. She imagined his strong mus-cled body under the baggy clothes. She flushed and closed her eyes.

"Are you all right?" Tama asked her.

"Yes."

"You sure?"

"Yes!"

"You're sweating." Tama said, turning on the air-conditioning.

Alice did not dignify this observation with an answer.

Mumbling, Tao asked if he could be dropped off downtown after the service.

"No!" said Tama, indignantly. She'd promised his parents that he wouldn't leave the house without her.

Poor Tao, almost as trapped as Alice. "I want… to go down-town, too," she said.

"See," said Tao, "even she wants to go."

Alice was pleased. He'd acknowledged her existence.

Tama shook her head. "I promised Alice's parents I'd bring her home right away."

"I'm not a baby," said Alice.

Tao laughed, a dark cackle that filled Alice with a fierce glow.

"I'm well aware of that," said Tama crisply.

But you're not, Alice thought.

They pulled into a scruffy strip mall. Alice had expected what she'd seen at the movies and on television—a tall steeple, wooden pews, stained glass windows—instead, they entered a plain beige storefront.

The room was full of big women in tight, bright clothes, and even bigger men smelling of strongly of cologne. There were rows of folding chairs, and a podium up front as though it were a classroom. Instead of a whiteboard behind the podium, there was a cross, and on the floor, a bucket with a dollar sign on it.

Tama moved a chair to make room for Alice's wheelchair and sat next to her with her hands folded and a bright look in her eyes. Alice, too, waited expectantly. Tao had disappeared. Perhaps he'd joined the other boys lurking near the door. She felt their maleness vibrating along her skin, raising the fine hairs on her arms.

The preacher, Brother Ford, with his white suit and comb-over, reminded Alice of the used-car dealer who appeared in advertisements on local TV. He spoke like the used-car dealer, too. Loudly and urgently, of hell and temptation and forgiveness, of souls leaving bodies. Of how if you accept Jesus Christ into your heart everything bad is washed away and you can begin again from scratch, like a newborn babe, only ten times better, a hundred times better!

When Brother Ford told the congregation to bow their heads and pray, Alice closed her eyes and silently asked for a lover. The God that Brother Ford spoke of seemed unlikely to grant this request, but since Alice didn't believe in Him, she thought she might as well believe in One who would.

Then she stopped listening, wondering what the boys behind her were thinking about. Had they noticed her? Her head lolled to the side the way it did when she was tired, and she forced it upright again at the thought that they might be watching.

Suddenly Brother Ford marched down the aisle, cupped Alice's shoulders roughly in his hands. "Dispel the demons that dwell within this poor creature!" he cried.

"In Christ's name, Amen!" shouted the congregation.

Tama whispered in her ear, "Don't worry. He's a healer."

Alice was startled but not frightened. The preacher roared commands, as if he was in charge of God. The congregation stamped their feet and cheered him on. They believed he could achieve a miracle, and, momentarily, so did Alice. Maybe her body was infested with demons, ones that played tricks with the muscles in her arms and legs, thickened her tongue, cackled as they destroyed her body.

Brother Ford pressed his sweaty hands against her ears. "Are you saved?" he cried.

"Don't know," Alice whispered.

"Patience," he said, looking at her grimly. He rushed off to someone else, an old woman near the front who gave a muffled cry and spit out what looked to Alice like chewing gum.

"Hallelujah!"

Some of the people he touched trembled, some moaned. Some called out, "Praise God!" while Alice sat quietly, perplexed because she felt exactly the same. Perhaps, as he'd said, she needed patience. He'd only touched her once.

After the service, lunch was served. Tama brought Alice a plate. Macaroni salad, slippery and thick with mayonnaise, and an oily mound of pork. The greasy morsels melted on Alice's tongue, her eyes rolled back with pleasure, the fatty food so different from the dull, wholesome meals her mother prepared, the brown rice, the grainy protein shakes. And just like that, part of Alice flew up her throat and out, a little gold bird, perched on the tip of her nose, joyfully surveying the world.

Neither Tama nor any of the others noticed anything. Alice, astonished, gestured at her nose and Tama plucked a tissue out of her purse and dabbed at Alice's nostrils. The bird, disturbed, and unobserved except by Alice, flew to the top of her head and sat in her hair.

Tama, sweat darkening her lime-green blouse, spooned coconut cream pie into Alice's mouth. She discreetly wiped Alice's cheek with a paper towel. "Brother has blessed you," Tama said, smiling. "What a tremendous day!"

It was a tremendous day. There was a hum in the air, Alice felt as though she was being lifted up and might even be propelled out of the wheelchair. The little gold bird studied the boys at the back of the room, who were working on plates piled high with rolls and pork. They were all large and healthy and loud.

Alice's bird flew across the room and landed on the back of Tao's chair. Unlike the others, he wasn't eating. He was telling a story. He needed to let the other boys know who he was and what he was capable of; only in this way did he feel safe. The story he told was different than what had actually happened; he could not allow himself to admit that he did not mean to do what he had done. He changed a few things, to make the story better.

The bird heard Tao saying, "…Don't mess with me, yo, and the sucker ran." The other boys murmured with admiration. But the bird saw that Tao was afraid and felt pity for him.

Alice was tired, her feet and hands beginning to twitch. She needed to use the restroom, to which she had to be helped. The bird returned, disappearing down her throat.

That was when Tama collapsed. One minute she was standing tall, the next she toppled. The chair in front of her fell with a clatter, the plate and pie sailed into the air.

Face down on the floor, Tama moaned, then she was silent. Alice prayed again, this time for Tama to please be okay. Brother Ford shouted for calm. Men rushed toward Tama and turned her over.

Alice's wheelchair was pushed to the side as a group gathered around Tama's unconscious body. One person lifted her wrist to feel her pulse. Alice saw Tao standing at the edge of the group, his arms dangling, his face astonished and guilty, as if he'd given Tama a push but hadn't expected her to fall.

The paramedics arrived. Tama, conscious now, a bruise rising on her temple, tried to speak but the words weren't coming out. She was strapped to a gurney and carried to the ambulance. A man handed Tao the keys to the van and sternly told him to drive Alice home.

Alice didn't dare look at Tao, shocked that one of her wishes had come true—that they would be alone together. Heart beating fast, she considered her situation. If Tao realized what he meant to her, he might despise her forever. Alice hadn't seen much of the world, but she had survived high school. Tao said nothing, just jingled the keys and cleared his throat before putting his hands to the wheelchair and pushing her out the door and into the hot summer air.

Soon Tao would have to touch her—buckling the seatbelt across her lap that was when. His hands might spring away, repelled, or they might linger, frighteningly, because now that his touch was a real possibility Alice was no longer sure she was ready. The worst would be if his touch was matter of fact. As if she wasn't a girl, just a thing. The way she'd heard the boys teasing in high school that time, on the field trip to the natural history museum, and how she'd had to pretend she hadn't heard.

They rolled without speaking down the concrete walkway, past a video store, supermarket, pharmacy, nail salon. Her parents and Tama always steered her around the bumpy spots but Tao pushed in a straight, fast line. The wheelchair jolted and jerked, the sun burned onto her hair and shoulders. Her arms and hands reddened, the sky was hazy white. Anything could happen, anything.

Tao didn't know how to work the lift that brought the wheel-chair up into the van. This gave Alice the opportunity to nod her head encouragingly. To say, "You almost have it." To smile. He didn't smile back.

Sparks when he buckled her. He was nervous and clumsy. He asked, "Is this too tight?"

"No, it's fine." This time Alice kept her face solemn, aware that her previous smile had been unsuccessful. He pressed the lever that shut the door and went around and climbed into the driver's seat.

The van idled while he spent some time absorbed in his phone. Alice hadn't thought to bring hers. There isn't much point when you're never alone. Now she wished she had it. She could bring it out. Busy herself. And what if they became friends? How else would they talk when apart?

Tao began to drive. They drove and drove, neither of them saying a word. After a while it became apparent that he wasn't taking her home. Her parents' fears came to her; all the jokes she'd overheard in high school. She felt a sickening draining sensation, as though all the blood in her body had slid to her feet. What she was more afraid of than anything else was that he would dump her somewhere and drive away.

"Where are we going?" Her arms spasmed. One smacked Tao's thigh. He flinched.

"Just a quick stop. All right? I'm not going to kidnap you."

Alice nodded, ashamed of her panic.

He took the exit for downtown.

"For a minute I thought Tama was dead." Tao said this so quietly it chilled Alice. She'd thought the same. She began to worry that by praying for a lover she'd caused Tama's collapse. No doubt answered prayers came with a price, although she was pretty sure hers hadn't even been answered yet. Her mother was a big believer in the power of the mind; for instance, there were cases of people curing themselves of cancer through meditation. Could you hurt someone with your thoughts without meaning to? She didn't know Tao well enough to discuss any of this. In fact, she didn't know anyone well enough. That in itself was a terrible thought.

"I hope she's okay," Tao said.

"Me, too," said Alice, sadly. She'd never seen Tama helpless. Never even seen her lying down before.

They were driving through a poor neighborhood. Alice could tell it was poor because, unlike the tidy street where she lived, there was trash everywhere. Some of the houses were boarded up. Tao pulled to the curb and tapped into his phone, muttering under his breath. Alice closed her eyes and tried to keep her breath even. Her chest felt as though it was full of thick syrup. Nothing to be done, she said to herself. She was good at waiting. She did it all the time.

Two boys appeared and Tao got out of the van. They bumped fists and elbows, huddled together. Alice pretended not to watch. It felt safest that way. To pretend disinterest. As if she drove around with Tao all the time.

The day was hot. Sweat trickled between her breasts. Sweat on her forehead, on her upper lip, between her legs. She still had to pee. She swiped her forehead with a hand and it came away glittery. Oh awful! No wonder he hadn't smiled back. No wonder he hadn't introduced her. She wondered how much of her face was smeared with gold eyeshadow. Like discovering dried snot hanging out your nose after class. She managed to look up and peer in the rearview mirror.

A shimmery smear across her forehead. She wiped with her hands until it was gone. But now her white skirt was stained. Dirty skirt. And she still didn't know where she was. Her parents might never let her leave the house again.

Tao got back into the van. He smelled strongly of something like burnt pine needles. "Okay then," he said, tucking the phone in his pants.

Again, they were driving. Tao was in a much better mood now, though his eyes were bloodshot. He turned on the radio and drummed his fingers on the steering wheel to the beat. He actually smiled, an exhilarating thing to witness.

The gold bird flew out her throat, perched in her hair, and told her what to say. "Where next?" she said.

Tao laughed. "You're so nice," he said. "You really are."

Alice looked out the window, annoyed. People always said this to her. As if she could help it. As if niceness was something she worked at. "Wish I wasn't," she said.

"Really? Hadn't thought of that."

"Nobody does."

Tao shrugged. "It's not a bad thing to be nice."

"Unless… you want to be bad."

His grin was nervous. He turned up the radio, then turned it down again. "You are sort of pretty."

Sort of! Why was what she imagined always better than what was real? She wished it could be the same for once. Just once. She looked away, out the window, at the world flying past. They were back on the freeway now. Presumably he was taking her home.

Tao drummed on the steering wheel, humming along. Tao wasn't nice. She knew that. She wasn't looking for nice because a nice boy would never think to touch her. Only bad boys crossed lines. Except maybe she was wrong. Maybe Tao was secretly nice, and only pretended to be bad, as boys did.

"Want to try something?" he said.

She shrugged.

"Ever smoked pot?"

"No," she said.

"Want to try?"

Yes, she did. The bird on top of her head began spinning like a firecracker. She was about to do something bad and that made her heart pound. She brimmed with joy.

"I hope this doesn't get me in trouble with your parents."

"It won't," she lied. Without a doubt, they were already in trouble, and they hadn't even done anything wrong yet.

They drove around until he found a scruffy little park with a deserted parking lot. He parked in the shade of a tree.

He smoked first, then put the joint to her lips and told her to inhale. She coughed and coughed. Her nose ran and she clumsily wiped it with her bare arm. Tao didn't seem to notice. The van was smoky, that pine-needle scent. His dark eyes closed.

"What do you think?"

Her chest hurt from coughing. Otherwise, she didn't feel much different. "It's great," she said. It wasn't a lie because what she meant was the whole thing, sitting here, with Tao, in the van, just the two of them.

"Check out the light coming down through the tree," he said. "Beautiful."

Alice hadn't noticed it. He was right, the green leaves almost black and in the gaps pure light.

"You are, too," he said, his tone regretful. "Beautiful. You're nice, too, just like my auntie. You're both so nice, and I'm not."

She flushed. He'd said the word 'beautiful.'

"You could be nice," she said, hesitantly, unsure this was the answer he wanted.

He leaned over and kissed her cheek. His lips were warm, dry, soft. Her cheek burned. She waited for more, her eyes closed, but he just started the van, rolled down the windows, and drove her home.

They didn't talk.

They didn't need to Alice felt, it would have been too much to say anything with her body so pink and warm and full of happiness. The gold bird sat on her shoulder and looked out the window at the summer world flashing by, beautiful, just as he'd said.

As Alice had expected, her parents were distraught. Where was Tama? Alice did her best to explain but that made it worse.

"Why didn't you call?" her mother said. "We would have come right away."

"You certainly should have called," her father repeated, as though Alice and Tao were both hard of hearing.

"I didn't have my phone," Alice said.

"And what about him? What about you, Tao?" her father said.

Tao shuffled his feet and ducked his head. He muttered something that might have been an apology but was impossible to hear, and then he got into Tama's beat-up sedan and drove off.

It suddenly struck Alice: she might never see him again.

"What happened?" her mother kept saying.

"Nothing!" Alice lied, weeping. "Nothing!"

"But why are you crying, Alice? You never cry."

"Tama," Alice said, which was partly true.

"Oh honey." They hugged her and kissed her, but these weren't the kisses she wanted, not at all.

"I need the bathroom," she sobbed and before she could stop herself the pee came out.

Her mother washed Alice's face and changed her out of the dirty skirt into a soft pair of sweatpants and brought her a cup of hot chocolate.

"Sweetheart," she said. "I think you should stay home for a few days. That outing was way too upsetting."

Alice didn't knock over the cup of hot chocolate on purpose, but she thought about it.

"Leave me alone," she said, afraid to say Tao's name. If she gave her parents even the slightest clue, they would know. They would say logical things, cautious things, things that seemed true. They would ruin everything.

Late that night, tucked into bed, Alice imagined Tao bringing her plates of macaroni salad, slipping bits of macaroni into her mouth. His strong fingers trailing down her blouse and over her breasts and down her belly, down, down, down. She rolled over, pressed onto her clenched hand, exploded softly again and again, and the golden bird flew up through the ceiling into the dark starry sky.

Tama had had a stroke. She could speak but her left side was weak. Later that week, Alice and her parents drove to visit her in the hospital. There were so many relatives in the room, so many large Samoans that anyone but Alice might have missed Tao, hidden in a corner, peering at his phone. He looked the same, the gigantic baggy jeans, the baggy white tee-shirt, his sturdy, soft face. When she caught his eye, he winked.

Alice's heart fluttered, and the golden bird flew out her throat. She'd been thinking about Tao constantly. His smooth, ashy skin, his dark eyes, the awkward way he had to hitch up his pants. "Hello," she mouthed. He gave her a small smile.

She smiled back and sent the bird over to perch on Tao's shoulder. The bird could read thoughts. Tao had been thinking about Alice, too. He thought her skin was beautiful and he liked her long hair, but he especially liked her niceness. Yes, he liked that she was nice! The one thing she didn't want to be.

Why didn't Tao come over to talk to her? This was a thought the gold bird couldn't read. Because Tao did not come over. Alice watched him. When she caught his eye, he shrugged and pointed to his phone, returning his attention to it. After a while, he put the phone in his pocket but still did not come.

It was the last time Alice saw him. Tama went home with her family the following week but wasn't strong enough anymore to work as an aide. She didn't come to see Alice again either.

Can you love someone who can't love you back? This was what Alice discovered to be true. She was very good at loving. She thought of Tao from sunrise to sundown, all sorts of thoughts. He had kissed her. He might come back some day. He might finally realize that she was the one. But in the hospital room he should have come over to talk, and he had not. There were two birds inside her now, one bright gold, and the other purple, dark as a bruise.

Skeleton Flower

Woody Woodger
—For Liv, and no one else

Hairless cats need sunscreen.
Like any other sentient, naked, muscle-pile
tossed to the elements, Sphinx
are susceptible to the sun, the internet

informs me. One particularly brave
Sphinx on Google Images

leans its wrinkled neck out over a blind-blue
pool. Besides allergens, dander,

brushing, one attraction I have to the Sphinx
is that, when furless, a cat's fingers
become exposed. No more mythical

paw, no softness. Just the sudden,
haunting realization
they've been copying
us the whole time,

more opposable than we thought.
How sweetly unsettling,

that a cat, at any point, could lace
its fingers in between yours,
copy that phalange weave previously

exclusive to humans.
Cat ladies everywhere will be thrilled. Finally! Contact.
Direct. Passionate.
Not mediated by their subsistence

to you, the manipulative way they mew.
Dogs will learn to shake, get slippers
smell my diabetes.

But a cat? A cat blinks
that slow, deliberate, fuck-you-and-the-fingers-

you-wrote-in-on and my heart uncorks,
shrivels as all the sappy nonsense leaks out.

Your fingers used to remind me of something
human, too. They might've

moved between mine, our rings loudly cuddled
together. Or they might've got lost
in me, my mouth or... elsewheres.

I'm not being polite for you but for me.

Remembering our skin together again,
mine wrung, shriveled, folds over bone,
snout pathetic, lowered into the dirt. So sorry.

Always. And yours conditional. Hungry.
So unfortunately familiar
and unpleasable—

a verse I could never unfold from the back
of my tongue. Today,

My friend likens me to the skeleton flower.
An Asian daffodil. Petit. Trampable.

She says when the rain soaks
them they grow transparent.
You can see them down to their veins.

You're like that, she says. *Imagine*

how beautiful you are to be like that.

I'm on the cusp of the verge of believing
her. She says, *goodness*

only comes of humility. And she's right—
I have misread humility
as loathing so many times
I've let the word chisel in scarlet

claw marks down my back. Flagellation
is only worth it if someone is watching.

And imagine how cunning, how lazy,
you have to be to just watch that. Purr.

Never blink. My friend and I both think everyone,
and that means you,
needs to bear our mistakes,
shave our sly fur and stand shivering,

fleshy fingers cupped in the rain.

Let's all meet grace together, our napes
cradled by the wide, black maw
of the universe. Our every wound

open, blanched, obvious,
unmistakable in the sun.

Amanda Moore *It's Hard to Cheat on Your Husband with Your Mother-in-law Living Two Doors Down*

Amanda Moore's poetry has appeared in journals and anthologies including *ZZYZVA, Cream City Review, Tahoma Literary Review, Best New Poets, and Mamas and Papas: On the Sublime and Heartbreaking Art of Parenting*, and she is the recipient of writing awards from The Writing Salon, Brush Creek Arts Foundation, and The Saltonstall Foundation for the Arts. Her essays have appeared or are forthcoming in *The Baltimore Review, Hippocampus Magazine*, and on the University of Arizona Poetry Center's blog, and she is a Contributing Poetry Editor at *Women's Voices for Change*. Currently a Board member for the Marin Poetry Center and 2019 Fellow at The Writers Grotto, Amanda is a high school teacher and lives by the beach in the Outer Sunset neighborhood of San Francisco with her husband and daughter. More at https://amandapmoore.com

"This piece comes from life, which is so often more unusual than anything I could think up in terms of narrative. I was particularly interested in recording how involved I was in the romantic liaisons of a neighbor without any of the direct players knowing of my involvement—it was a new level on illicit, intrusive, and dishonest in its own way."

Bryan Shawn Wang *Anachronisms*

Bryan Shawn Wang lives in Berks County, Pennsylvania. A former research scientist, he teaches biochemistry at Penn State Berks but also has a long-standing interest in literature. His stories have appeared in *Potomac Review, Gulf Stream, Washington Square, Valparaiso Fiction Review*, and *Kenyon Review Online*.

"It's the summer of 2019, and my son and I are on The College Tour, visiting campuses with pretty brick buildings and campuses with pretty stone buildings and campuses with pretty concrete buildings. (Okay, tidy and functional concrete buildings.) We see urban schools, schools with city skylines on the horizon, schools in idyllic towns nestled in the mountains, atop rolling hills, overlooking gorgeous lakes. He finds the journey intriguing, inspiring at times, and a bit intimidating. I'm overcome with a profound and persistent case of wistfulness, each stop another dose of nostalgia and melancholy. I long for my own undergraduate days, when I had no net worth, no responsibilities, no perspective, but I had an abundance of optimism and potential. My inner nerd yearns for life as a student. And for instruction: in school, there was instruction, and there were *instructions*, direct and explicit paths to affirmation, accolade. I marvel at the array of academic options presented to my son, options I hadn't recognized, much less explored, during my own college search. (How many of us in those days conducted anything like a college "search"?) How might my life have differed—and how might it not have differed—had I looked beyond Dear Old State and enrolled in a school with an open curriculum or an exploratory program, a place that valued the arts and humanities alongside the sciences, that appreciated, even encouraged, interdisciplinary thinking?

"But I hadn't. And when two roads diverge, no matter which is chosen, the other must be left untaken.

"The creeping dread and remorse intensifies as I consider my son's tightrope walk toward independence. Because he's shaky and naïve and myopic. Because, in some respects, he still seems a toddler—cranky one minute and adorable the next. He takes a substantial nap most afternoons; some days, several naps. He's selfish and heedless. He demands space in my house, in my schedule, in my attention out of proportion to even his grown (not to say grown-up) self. Just a short time ago, this child for the first time was rising to stand on his own two feet. This child is teetering on the cusp of adulthood. I'm to entrust him to the care of some pimply Resident Assistant, a nattering advisor in a cluttered office, a cadre of distracted professors? To an *institution*, no matter how polished and punctilious and progressive? This boy is about to leave my house and seek his fortune? I've tried to advise him, discipline him, encourage him, challenge him. Was it enough? I've tried to show and tell him how much I love him. He's rolling his eyes. He takes out his air pods and takes his car keys from the hook. Where's he going? Out. With whom? The guys. When will he be back? The door shuts.

"His wallet's still on the counter."

Carolyn Martin *Lost & Found in the Universe*

From associate professor of English to management trainer to retiree, **Carolyn Martin** has journeyed from New Jersey through California to Oregon to discover Douglas firs, months of rain, and dry summers. Her poems and book reviews have appeared in publications throughout North America, Australia, and the UK, and her fourth collection, *A Penchant for Masquerades*, was released by Unsolicited Press in 2019. She is currently the poetry editor of *Kosmos Quarterly: journal for global transformation*. Find out more about Carolyn at www.carolynmartinpoet.com.

"Two of my favorite sources of inspiration collided to create this poem. The first is my partner of 27-years who has provided me with a wealth of material for a number of poems as well as quotable lines I could never make up. 'I can hear you roll your eyes' is one of them. The second: scientific articles that offer richly poetic images like those that fill the third stanza. In addition, I had just read an article that claimed that the center of the galaxy '*tastes/ like raspberries and smells like rum.*' Again, I couldn't create livelier images than these scientists. Put these two sources together and the result is 'Lost & Found in the Universe.'"

Catherine Edmunds *Small Creatures*

Catherine Edmunds is a prolific writer, artist, and fiddle player with award nominated Irish folk/rock band 'Share the Darkness'. Her published written works include two poetry collections, four novels and a Holocaust memoir. She has been nominated three times for a Pushcart Prize, shortlisted in the Bridport four times, and has works in journals including *Aesthetica, Crannóg* and *Ambit*. Catherine lives in North-East England between the High Pennines and the grey North Sea. *twitter.com/CathyEdmunds* and *www.facebook.com/catherine.edmunds*

"The genesis of 'Small Creatures' lay initially in having witnessed some particularly messy and tragic roadkill and wondering whether I would have the courage to put an end to the suffering of a severely injured animal myself. This led to me exploring the nature and psychology of someone who had sought out damaged creatures from childhood, and what the implications might be for his future partner, given that a pattern of sociopathic behaviour in adults is often directly related to how they treated or mistreated animals as children. The love between the two adults in this story is dangerously skewed by their individual personalities. Once I had invented them and set them on a path, their fates took an inevitable course. This is how I tend to write. Invent a couple of characters. Set them a problem. See what they do."

Charles Watts *Knocking Off Corners*

Charlie Watts earned an MFA from Brown University studying with writers including Meredith Steinbach, Robert Coover, and Michael Ondaatje. Charlie has published stories in journals including *Carve, CRAFT, Narrative, Storm Cellar,* and *Sequestrum.* He and his wife, a chaplain, live in rural New Hampshire after other lives in Boston and Providence.

"My wife and I got married when we were twenty-two. We told my parents—from whom we expected some stiff resistance—that, because we were so young, we could grow up together. We said, this will make us strong and inseparable. They smiled. We thought we'd gotten away with something. And while our theory has been largely correct (34 years so far), we grossly miscalculated the degree of difficulty. This poem tries to celebrate that struggle and the delicate gift of everyday unbroken things. For the record, my parents had absolutely no objections to our marriage."

Corrie Haldane *At Last and Too Soon*

Corrie Haldane spends her days wrangling numbers but enjoys playing with words at night. Her work has appeared in magazines such as *More of Our Canada* and *Lifestyles Magazine,* and her short fiction has been included in several print anthologies, including *Renaissance: Short Fiction* as selected by Sarah Selecky, *Little Bird Stories, vol. 5,* and *Wordplay 2013.* Corrie lives in Newmarket, Ontario, Canada with her two sons.

"A bubble bath, a Spotify playlist, and an active imagination—that's where my story, 'At Last and Too Soon', was born. 'We're Going To Be Friends' by the White Stripes, 'Steamroller' by Phoebe Bridgers, and 'Oceans' by Seafrot played in just the right order and at just the right time. Nick and Tara's relationship emerged through the music and the steam; I got out of the tub and wrote it all down."

D. Dina Friedman *Love*

D. Dina Friedman has received two Pushcart Prize nominations and published in many literary journals including *Lilith, Negative Capability, The Sun, Common Ground Review, San Pedro River Review, Steam Ticket, New Plains Review, Blue Stem, Red Booth Review, Bloodroot, Anderbo,* and *Rhino.* Dina is also the author of two award-winning young adult novels, *Escaping Into the Night* (Simon and Schuster) and *Playing Dad's Song* (Farrar, Straus, Giroux) and one chapbook of poetry, *Wolf in the Suitcase* (Finishing Line Press). Dina moved with her husband to western Massachusetts 38 years ago because it was "a compromise between Brooklyn and the Ozarks." She currently lives in Hadley, next door to a farm with 500 cows. She has an MFA from Lesley University and teaches at the University of Massachusetts/Amherst. To learn more about Dina, visit her website at www.ddinafriedman.com.

"As an immigration justice activist, I keep hearing so many human stories about families and loved ones torn apart by circumstance. This story is one of what I hope will soon be a collection of short fiction exploring how immigration affects all of us in so many subtle and compelling ways. The initial scene came to me on a walk, as did the idea to set the locale by the library that really does straddle Vermont and Canada, but it took a while to figure out who these characters really were, and the story took more than a year to develop. In its early versions, the story ended with ICE coming to the door, but every single person who gave me feedback wanted to know what happened. I realized that sad as it might be, I had to go on and follow Roberto and Shanti's deeper-than-realized love to its bittersweet and inevitable end."

Dallas Woodburn *In the Lemon Orchard*

Dallas Woodburn is author of the short story collection *Woman, Running Late, in a Dress* (Yellow Flag Press) and the novel *The Best Week That Never Happened* (Month9Books). Her honors and awards include a John Steinbeck Fellowship in Creative Writing, four Pushcart Prize nominations, first place in the international Glass Woman Prize, and second place in the American Fiction Prize. Her short stories have appeared in *Cicada*, *ZYZZYVA*, *The Nashville Review*, *Fourth River*, and *Monkeybicycle*, among many others. Dallas is also a book writing coach (www.yourbookbreakthrough.com) and the founder of Write On! Books (writeonbooks.org), an organization that empowers youth through reading and writing endeavors.

"I first drafted 'In the Lemon Orchard' as a graduate student at Purdue University, pursuing my MFA in Fiction. Originally the story was written in third person rather than first person. We were reading Arundhati Roy's gorgeous novel *The God of Small Things* at the time, which inspired me to relax and play with language, and not try to hold a story so tightly in my fists. At the time I wrote this piece, I was living in Indiana—a stark contrast to my California hometown—and the distance gave me a fresh perspective on a place I knew so intimately. When writing 'In the Lemon Orchard,' I began with setting and let the characters and plot grow outward from there. I had no idea about the end of the story until I wrote the final scene. It was a discovery for me as much as I hope it is for the reader."

Dennis Mombauer *Kairoi*

Dennis Mombauer currently lives in Colombo as a consultant on climate change and writer of speculative fiction, textual experiments, and poetry. He has published fiction and nonfiction in various magazines and anthologies, and his first English novel, *The Fertile Clay*, will be published by Nightscape Press in late 2020.

"'Kairoi' attempts to capture a fleeting moment from three perspectives: those of a man, a woman, and an outside observer who may not be able to spot any difference between the first two. Nothing extraordinary happens, they are just two people meeting in a hotel lobby, but perspective and perception still make a huge difference."

Ellaraine Lockie *Brotherhood of the Midnight Snack*

Ellaraine Lockie's recent work has won the 2019 *Poetry Super Highway* Contest, the Nebraska Writers Guild's Women of the Fur Trade Poetry Contest and *New Millennium's Monthly Muse-paper* Poetry Contest. Her fourteenth chapbook, *Sex and Other Slapsticks*, has been released from Presa Press. Earlier collections won Poetry Forum's Chapbook Contest Prize, San Gabriel Valley Poetry Festival Chapbook Competition, Encircle Publications Chapbook Contest, Best Individual Poetry Collection Award from *Purple Patch Magazine in England* Competition, and the Aurorean's Chapbook Choice Award. Her poems have found their ways onto broadsides, buses, rented cars, bicycles, cabins, greeting cards, key chains, bookmarks, mugs, coffee sack labels, church bulletins, radio shows and cable TV as well as into hundreds of national and international journals, magazines and anthologies. Thirty of her poems have been nominated for Pushcart Prizes, and she has received multiple writing fellowship awards from both Summer Literary Seminars and Centrum Literary Residencies. Ellaraine teaches writing workshops and serves as Poetry Editor for the lifestyles magazine, *LILIPOH*.

"My brother, my only sibling and ten years older than I, was also my best friend for as long as I can remember. I was devastated from his death. I waited for time to fill the void that he left and to fan the anger from a faulty medical system that burned inside me. But it wasn't until I began writing about him that I found acceptance and a place of peace. Resurrecting him through poetry and memoir has become not only a type of therapy but a way to share the unique person he was with other people—my readers. 'Brotherhood of the Midnight Snack,' is one of these sharings."

Emerson Tenney *In Tenderness and Faith*

Emerson Tenney is a California-born poet currently residing in New York City. An emerging writer, Emerson received her BA in Literary Arts from Brown University in the spring of 2020. In addition to exploring narrative through experimental fiction, Emerson also works as a screenwriter. She made her directorial debut in the summer of 2019 with a short film she wrote entitled, "The First Few Days." Public release will follow festival season this spring.

"While writing for the Darkhouse anthology, *What We Talk About When We Talk About It*, I found myself thinking, what are the classic love stories we tell again and again throughout generations? There is the hero and the damsel, the best friend suddenly discovered as the true love all along, there is the heartbreak of love unrequited... all of these loves, romantic. However, the more I thought about it, the more I realized this was a very narrow view of what constitutes a love story. One story often overlooked, or at least relegated to a genre other than Love, is that of the archetypal relationship between mother and child. Throughout 'In Tenderness and Faith,' I hope to explore and complicate the circular bond between mother and daughter, the delicate dance between safety and suffocation, and the shapes we make in search of independence."

Emily Rapp Black *End*

Emily Rapp Black Emily Rapp Black is the author of *Poster Child: A Memoir*, and *The Still Point of the Turning World*. She has two books forthcoming in 2021: *Sanctuary* (Random House), and *Frida Kahlo and My Left Leg* (Nottinghill Editions/New York Review of Books). A former Fulbright scholar, she is the recipient of Guggenheim Fellowship. She is Associate Professor of Creative Writing at the University of California-Riverside. She lives in the Inland Empire.

Erika Rasmussen *In the Dust*

Erika Rasmussen was born and grown in Colorado. Her growth continued at Santa Clara University, where she graduated in the spring of 2020 with degrees in English and sociology. For the next year, she will work as an O'Hare Fellow with America magazine. She knows very few things in life, except that she wants to love, to create, and to understand—and is figuring out how to do that one step at a time.

"I really did feel that solidarity with dust. It's common knowledge by now that 'we are all made of stardust,' and even the dust accumulating on our old books and picture frames and stagnant shapes is a piece of the very living ecosystem of the universe. Something smaller than us, something that we look like next to the sun. And it's relentless. I want to be that—relentless. There is no other way in this life. But while dust does not choose to be relentless, we have to choose it. I'm relentlessly clinging to what feels like home. As I grow, this home grows smaller and smaller, it seems. Truth and love—not to be confused as simple structures—are my home right now. I want to accumulate there."

Evan L. Balkan *The School Bus No Longer Stops in Front of the House*

Evan L. Balkan is the author of three novels, Including the PEN/ Faulkner nominated *Independence*, and seven books of nonfiction, including *The Wrath of God: Lope de Aguirre, Revolutionary of the Americas*, as well as many essays and short stories in an array of publications. His screenplay *Spitfire*, adapted from his novel of the same name, won the 2016 Baltimore Screenwriters Competition, a Saul Zaentz Innovation Fund Fellowship, a Rocaberti scholarship, and was a semifinalist in the Screencraft Family Friendly Screenwriting Competition as well as a finalist for an ISA fellowship; his screenplays *Children of Disobedience* and *King of the Freaks* have also won multiple fellowships and awards. He is a co-writer for the television series, *Wayward Girls*. He coordinates the English Department at the Community College of Baltimore County, where he runs the creative writing program, and is an adjunct faculty member in the Johns Hopkins University's graduate Teaching Writing program. He holds degrees in the humanities from Towson, George Mason, and Johns Hopkins universities and has served as a guest lecturer at Yale, Johns Hopkins, Bryn Mawr, and many other institutions.

"I am interested in how men navigate relationships in a climate in which many of the old masculine tropes are, appropriately, being challenged and altered. There remains a tension between the thrust toward masculinity in its positive manifestations and the idea that any reflection or assertion of masculinity is inherently retrograde. I take no strong position here, but rather like to work in fiction with male characters who—subconsciously—struggle within those tensions."

Flo Golod *Your Sweet Voice Calling*

Flo Golod lives in south Minneapolis. She is married to Scott Bartell. A retired non-profit consultant, mother and grandmother, she's active in the Master Gardener Program. Her stories have appeared in two issues of *Talking Stick* (one received a second-place award), the 2018 *Choices* anthology from Temptation Press, and the online journals, *Manifestations*. This story originally appeared in *BoomerLit Mag (boomerlitmag.com):Fall 2016*.

"I fell in love at fifty and discovered that building a relationship late in life is no easier than when one is young. Somewhere in that middle-aged coming together, this story was born. The title is a phrase lifed from "Not The Only One" by Bonnie Riatt."

Jack Mackey *Today I Bought New Cutlery*

Jack Mackey lives in Southern Delaware. He holds a master's degree in English from the University of Maryland. His poetry has been anthologized by Darkhouse Books (*Descansos*) and the Rehoboth Beach Writers' Guild. Poems have appeared in *Mojave River Review, Rat's Ass Review, Mobius, Writer's Resist, Third Wednesday, Anti-Heroin Chic, The Broadkill Review,* and others.

"In this poem I'm try to capture the grief experienced at the end of a marriage—the end of love—that began when you were young and only needed a few things to make a home."

Jackie Craven *Postcards I Wish I'd Sent Lisbeth When We Were Girls*

Jackie Craven is the author of *Secret Formulas & Techniques of the Masters* (Brick Road Poetry Press, 2018) and a chapbook, *Our Lives Became Unmanageable* (Omnidawn, 2016), winner of Omnidawn's Fabulist Fiction Award. Her poems have appeared in *The Massachusetts Review, Nimrod, New Ohio Review, River Styx*, and many other journals and anthologies. www.JackieCraven.com

"The whimsical 'postcards' in this poem evolved from a prompt created by poet Jim Simmerman and published in the exercise book, *The Practice of Poetry* (Robin Behn and Chase Twichell, eds.). To encourage a sense of play, Simmerman listed 'Twenty Little Poetry Projects' designed to break boundaries of language and logic. For example: 'Say something specific but utterly preposterous' and 'Modify a noun with an unlikely adjective.' After completing the exercise, I had twenty wacky responses to toy with. A child's voice emerged and I began to think of my own childhood in Northern Virginia. Oh, those steamy summers! Those brutal heartbreaks! There really were unruly hollyhocks, leashed dogs spinning in dirt yards, and stinging rejections from a girl who used to be my comrade in mischief. Casting the poem as a series of imaginary postcards offered a way to speak directly to 'Lisbeth' and also to set the scenes in the early 1960s. 'Postcards I Wish I'd Sent Lisbeth' has previously appeared in *The Fourth River* (Spring 2015) and the *World Enough Writers* anthology, *Ice Cream Poems* (Summer 2017)."

Jason Arias *What We Talk on When We Trip at Rock Quarries*

Jason Arias lives in Portland, OR. His debut short story collection Momentary Illumination of *Objects in Motion* was published in 2018 by Black Bomb Books. His writing has appeared in *NAILED Magazine, The Nashville Review, Oregon Humanities Magazine, Perceptions Magazine*, Lidia Yuknavitch's *The Misfit's Manifesto*, and many other places. To find more of Jason's writing and future readings visit JasonAriasAuthor.com.

"In the story 'What We Talk on When We Trip at Rock Quarries' I wanted to explore how we confront uncertainty; how our minds are always at play, trying to normalize, desensitize, and manipulate our fears and frailty into something manageable and knowable. I wanted to play with impulsivity as a means of control. I wanted to look at thought patterns and perception. And by the end of this exercise I only had more questions. I ended up wondering what all the term altered state of mind included. Are love, fear, loneliness and laughter all altered states?"

Jenn Richter *After the Fight*

Jenn Richter has been published in *Blue Collar Review, Shakespeare's Monkey Revue*, and various anthologies. She has a B.A. in writing/literature from George Fox University and works as the Early Learning Program Manager in McMinnville, Oregon, where she lives with her husband and family. In her spare time, she likes to read, write and kayak.

"'After the Fight' attempts to capture the quiet rage of a woman who has to keep it together for her family—and the tension in a home where no one will speak about what everyone already knows."

Jesse Sensibar *Retired Speedfreak Chopper Rider*

Jesse Sensibar loves small furry animals and assault rifles with equal abandon and has a soft spot in his heart for innocent strippers and jaded children. He has worked as a mechanic, heavy equipment operator, strip club bouncer, repossession agent, tattoo shop owner, private investigator, tow truck driver, snowplow operator, wildland firefighter, and college English teacher. He spends his time writing and promoting the art of storytelling. You can usually find him in the dying Ponderosa Pine forests surrounding Flagstaff, Arizona or in the old barrios of Tucson, Arizona. Otherwise, he is probably somewhere out on the highway, documenting the passing of his rapidly disappearing American West and pondering the fleeting nature of memory, sin, spirituality, and forgiveness.

"I wrote this piece in the years when I was first sober after a lifetime spent wrapped up in Southwestern outlaw drug culture. If you're not sure what that is think Breaking Bad except the dead do not get to get up and go on to star in another show. One of the most tragic things about my own addiction, to me at least, was the loss of both feeling and memory, one of the great things about drugs for me was the numbness they created, my ability not to feel was my greatest asset in the drug world. Once I got sober, I realized it was also my greatest loss. This piece addresses that in the most visceral way I could come up with at the time that I wrote it."

James M. LeCuyer *First Love*

Jim LeCuyer was born in Los Angeles and raised next to the ocean in Long Beach, California. He holds an MA in Creative Writing from San Francisco State University, another in Clinical Psychology from the San Francisco Graduate School of Psychology, and one in Education from the University of California. Besides two short story collections, *Threnody for Sturgeon*, and *Duck Lessons* (Darkhouse Books), he has published a book of poetry, *A Brick for Offissa Pupp* (Floating Island Press) as well as various poems in newspapers and magazines. He served as a junior officer in the Navy, worked fifteen years as a commercial fisherman, and for some twenty-five years, taught English literature and creative writing at various high schools in the San Francisco Bay Area, including Albany, Oakland Tech, Woodrow Wilson, and San Francisco School of the Arts. He was a member of Marin Artists for Social Responsibility, and is a board member of *Poetry Flash*, as well as former Chair of the Non-Fiction Committee of the Northern California Book Awards. He has been active in the effort to eliminate high-stakes testing in public schools, and has worked to establish an environmental contest within the San Francisco Unified School District. He presently lives in Fremont, California. You can reach him at jameslecuyer@yahoo.com.

"The motive for the story? Well, it was a first kiss. Not many first kisses have such a result, and even fewer relationships develop afterwards. It's a pretty traditional first date story other than that, a slow awakening to sensual possibilities. It's not such a pretty story, but I don't seem to be interested in the pretty, probably a major failing on my part. It took place almost exactly seventy years ago, but it's still fresh and amazing to me. What has happened since is also amazing, but I doubt my ability to tell it, for much of it is very painful. In another seventy or so years, I'll forgive myself enough to get it all down. Do they still publish True Confessions?"

John Guzlowski

John Guzlowski's writing appears in *Rattle, North American Review, Main Street Rag*, and other journals. *Echoes of Tattered Tongues*, his memoir about his parents' experiences as slave laborers in Nazi Germany, won the Benjamin Franklin Poetry Award and the Eric Hoffer/Montaigne Award. His most recent book of autobiographical poems is *True Confessions*. He is also the author of the Hank and Marvin mystery novels (reviewed in the *New York Times*) and a columnist for the *Dziennik Zwiazkowy*, the oldest Polish daily newspaper in the US.

"It was a bad summer. We were living in a small town in Central Illinois in a county known primarily for farming. The rain stopped in early May and didn't come back until fall. The farmers would watch their crops dying, and although we weren't farmers, we felt the despair they were feeling. I was teaching that summer, and one of the books I was teaching was John Steinbeck's novel of the Great Depression, *The Grapes of Wrath*. I would look around and see the crops shriveling up and dying and I couldn't help but thinking this dying would never end, that the suffering Steinbeck described would be soon upon us all. And I wondered how we would get through it. My daughter Lillian showed me the way. She had an optimism and a strength and a love of everything that showed me that—no matter what—people would pull through."

Kat Hausler *Separation*

Originally from Virginia, **Kat Hausler** is a graduate of New York University and holds an MFA in Fiction from Fairleigh Dickinson University, where she was the recipient of a Baumeister Fellowship. She is a translator and author of the novel *Retrograde*. Her work has appeared in *34th Parallel, Inkspill Magazine, Rozlyn Press, Porridge Magazine, LitReactor, BlazeVOX*, and *The Airgonaut*, among others. She lives in Berlin. "Separation" first appeared in *Rozlyn: Short Fiction by Women Writers*.

"Regarding the setup, I remember having recently read a Nabokov story where a man puts a fake skeleton in bed with his sleeping wife. Obviously that story has a much lighter tone, but it certainly called the idea of a rude awakening to mind. Other than that, I drew inspiration from relationship troubles—my own and other people's—Sleeping Beauty, and Berlin."

Kathleen Hayes Phillips *He Wanted His Ashes Scattered in Ireland*

Kathleen Hayes Phillips has found great joy in putting words on paper. A widow, mother, grandmother and retired teacher, Katy (as she is called), lives and writes in a senior residence. When not at her desk overlooking a busy Milwaukee street, she is out exploring the old and new in the city that has been home for a lifetime.

Katy's poetry and creative nonfiction can be read online and in many publications, her latest work in *Nature's Healing Spirit*, WFOP's *Bramble* and *The Poets' Calendar, and Van Gogh Dreams* published by Henschell-Haus Publishing.

Lisa Dordal *Induction*

Lisa Dordal teaches in the English Department at Vanderbilt University and is the author of *Mosaic of the Dark*, which was a finalist for the 2019 Audre Lorde Award for Lesbian Poetry. She is a Pushcart Prize nominee and the recipient of an Academy of American Poets University Prize, the Robert Watson Poetry Prize and the Betty Gabehart Poetry Prize. Her poetry has appeared in *Best New Poets, Ninth Letter, CALYX, The Greensboro Review, Vinyl Poetry, and Nasty Women Poets: An Unapologetic Anthology of Subversive Verse*. Her website is lisadordal.com.

"This poem was inspired by a photograph taken of me on Christmas Eve when I was fourteen. In the photo, I am drinking from a bottle of sangria that had been given to me for Christmas by my mother. I had a memory of this experience but finding the photograph made it that much more real. It seems so unlikely that a mother would give her teenage daughter a six-pack of sangria, but now there was no way I could deny this happened. The poem is called "Induction" because this seems to have been exactly what my mother was doing (consciously or not): inducting me into the ways of drinking just as her own mother had inducted her. It's as if she wanted company, someone to share her pastime with. And I was the one she chose."

Lisa Masé *First Cold*

Lisa Masé is a poet, folk herbalist, nutritionist and food sovereignty activist from Italy. She now lives and homesteads in Vermont with her partner and two children. Her poems have been most recently published by *Press 53*, the *Long Island Review*, and *Red River Press*.

"I write from my observations of food, family, and geography. I wrote this poem when my daughter caught her first cold at 8 months of age. The meeting of autumn melancholy and the struggle of watching a child get their first illness inspired these words."

Lita Kurth *Heart, River*

Lita Kurth holds an MFA from Pacific Lutheran University, has published in three genres in numerous journals and anthologies. "Are We Not Ladies," was nominated by Watershed Review for Best of the Net, 2017. "This is the Way We Wash the Clothes," (CNF) won the 2014 Diana Woods Memorial Award (Lunchticket). Her creative nonfiction "Pivot," and short story, "Gardener's Delight" (Dragonfly Press DNA) were nominated for Pushcart Prizes. A sampling of publications: *The Millions, Atticus Review, Brain,Child, Main Street Rag, Microfiction Monday*. In 2013, she co-founded San Jose's Flash Fiction Forum, a popular reading series.

"'Heart, River' is a story based on facts, a re-creation of the way my friend lost her husband. It was originally published in *DNA Dragonfly Press*, 2015."

LM Harrod *Seated Couple*

Lois Marie Harrod's latest collection *Woman* was published by Blue Lyra in February 2020. *Her Nightmares of the Minor Poet* appeared in June 2016 from Five Oaks; her chapbook *And She Took the Heart* appeared in January 2016; *Fragments from the Biography of Nemesis* (Cherry Grove Press) and the chapbook *How Marlene Mae Longs For Truth* (Dancing Girl Press) appeared in 2013. A Dodge poet, she is published in literary journals and online ezines from *American Poetry Review* to *Zone 3*. Links to her online work http://www.loismareharrod.org.

"I was inspired by Egon Schiele's painting of the same name"

Marilyn Horn *The Killer Instinct*

Marilyn Horn (marilynhornwriting.com) works as a technical editor in Silicon Valley. Her short stories have appeared in *Marathon Review, Blotterature, and NonBinary Review*, among others, and she also reads at San Jose's Flash Fiction Forum from time to time. *Beyond the Fence*, a collection of her stories, is available from Thinking Ink Press (thinkinginkpress.com).

"I'm fascinated and annoyed and sometimes frightened by the voices in my head. I spend a lot of time sorting them out and wondering how they got there and trying not to let them steer me in the wrong direction. This story sprang up as I was thinking about how, if we're lucky, we can choose which voices to listen to. That led to the realization that not all of us have that capacity, so then I wondered about what that must be like—not being able to control the voices in your head, and the strategies you might come up with in response to that. There was never a dark ending to this story as I developed it; for Carleen and Bud, I knew love would win in the end."

Mary Maddox *What Love Is*

Mary Maddox is a horror and dark fantasy novelist with what *The Charleston Times-Courier* calls a "Ray Bradbury-like gift for deft, deep-shadowed description." Born in Soldiers Summit, high in the mountains of Utah, Maddox graduated with honors in creative writing from Knox College, and went on to earn an MFA from the University of Iowa Writers' Workshop. She taught writing at Eastern Illinois University and has published four novels. Her stories have appeared in various journals, including *Yellow Silk, Farmer's Market, The Scream Online*, and *Huffington Post*. The Illinois Arts Council has honored her fiction with a Literary Award and an Artist's Grant. Visit her online at marymaddox.com.

"'What Love Is' grew from my early childhood in Soldiers Summit, Utah. The town was mostly ruins, the wooden husks and concrete foundations of railroad housing and a few commercial buildings, decaying in the dust and sagebrush. My father, like Dee's, worked as a dispatcher at the railroad depot there. My brother and I played with two brothers who lived next door. Mickey and his brother are based on them. Our mothers became friends and stayed in touch after they left Soldiers Summit. Both women ended up divorcing their husbands. Although I saw the boys every so often, there was no puppy love between me and either one of them. Their mother died of cancer when the younger boy was seventeen, and he shot himself soon afterward. I can only guess why. Grief for his mother, feelings of abandonment and despair. Soldiers Summit has kept a lasting hold on my imagination. For years I dreamed of the place regularly—lonely, haunting dreams.

Another inspiration for the story was my strong emotional response to smells. Even after decades, certain smells evoke the circumstances around them—the catsup and eggs my father was eating when he quarreled with my mother at breakfast, the diesel fumes in the bus station when my brother and I traveled between one parent and the other, the alcoholic breath of a boy whose kiss I did not welcome.

I wonder whether love begins—or dies—with a response to the way someone smells and to other cues that register unconsciously. I wonder whether Evening in Paris, or any other perfume, can disguise the truth for long."

Mary Silwance *(you already else where)*

Mary Silwance Mary Silwance mothers three daughters, is a poet and environmental writer and speaker. Her work appears in numerous publications and on her blog, Tonic Wild, where she addresses the spiritual and justice aspects of environmental issues. She is a 2019 recipient of the Bread Loaf-Rona Jaffe Foundation Scholarship for environmental non-fiction. When not writing, you can find her outside.

"The poem was inspired by my changing relationship with my oldest daughter. It's a reflection on the details that connect us now that she's a teen contrasted with the details that connected us when she was a preschooler."

MeeRee Orlandini *Zugzwang*

MeeRee Orlandini is a poet and fiction writer based in Philadelphia. She received her BFA in Creative Writing from the University of the Arts. By day, she is an assistant first grade teacher at Germantown Friends School.

"Zugzwang is a term used in chess to describe a situation in which a player must take their turn but all possible moves put them at a disadvantage. Zugzwang is when you are forced to do something that you don't want to do. I wrote this poem about a really difficult relationship I was in, where my partner became my constant opponent. This poem is about watching yourself get weaker even in the smartest game. It's about denial and all the corners you have to turn in a day, about getting fed up with the rules, and finally learning how to make your own. I just learned that the word zugzwang is German for 'compulsion to move.' I'm glad I ate the bishop."

Mel Carlson *Waipahu*

Mel Carlson worked at *Poetry Magazine* while he attended Northwestern University on the GI bill. Throughout the 1950s and early 1960s he wrote drama and docudrama for public broadcasting and the CBC in Canada. Subsequently, he taught film writing and aesthetics in the Film Department at San Francisco State University before retiring in 1988. His short story, "Walking on Water", was published in *Tin House, volume 26*.

"Shortly after Pearl Harbor, I enlisted in the US Army and was assigned to an S2 (combat intelligence) section. We trained in Hawaii prior to our service in New Guinea and the Philippines where we ran patrols behind Japanese lines. Cletus is modeled on one of the soldiers in our six-man group. By common agreement, the other five left him in camp to draw maps from aerial photographs rather than to risk our lives on the chance he'd fuck up a patrol."

Morrow Dowdle *The Ride*

Morrow Dowdle is a poet living in Hillsborough, NC. She released her first chapbook, *Nature v. Nurture* (Artagem Graphic Library) in 2018. She has published poetry in numerous journals and anthologies, most recently *The Baltimore Review, Adanna Literary Journal, Poetry South, Dandelion Review,* and *Panoply*. She was a Pushcart Prize nominee in 2018. She is a member of the North Carolina Poetry Society and the Living Poetry collective of the North Carolina Triangle area. She also writes graphic novels in collaboration with her husband, Max Dowdle, including *An Unlikely Refugee*, a collaboration with the North Carolina Museum of Natural Sciences, which now houses a permanent exhibit related to the book. She currently works as a physician assistant in mental healthcare.

"'The Ride,' like many poems, is based on a simple event from my life that led me down an imaginative path to deeper insight. I come from a family suffering from multigenerational addiction, mental illness, and interpersonal abuse. I wasn't sure whether I would ever have children because I didn't want to bring them into those circumstances. However, when I had my daughter, I experienced a sense of mutual love and personal healing that I didn't know was possible. Looking at 'The Ride' almost two years after writing it, I see it now as a song of hope for my family in general and also something of a hymn to my daughter in particular."

Neil Brosnan *Company*

Neil Brosnan is an Irish author and songwriter. A winner of The Bryan MacMahon, and Ireland's Own short story awards, his stories have appeared in magazines, anthologies, and electronic format in Ireland, Britain, Europe, and the USA. He has published two collections: *Fresh Water & Other Stories* (Original Writing, 2010) and *Neap Tide & Other Stories* (New Binary Press, 2013). https://sites.google.com/site/neilbrosnanwrites/https://www.facebook.com/neil.brosnan1

"This is the story of a sixteen-year-old girl who is suddenly responsible for an ageing father, a new-born brother, and the running of the family farm when her mother dies in childbirth. As years go by, she has to cope with all the demands of adulthood having never had the chance to live a life of her own."

Paula Rudnick *Patricide*

Paula Rudnick is a former TV producer whose credits range from late night rock and roll shows to Emmy-nominated movies for television. After retiring from the entertainment industry, she became a political activist and served on numerous non-profit boards, among them The Geffen Playhouse, MOCA, Sarah Lawrence College and Planned Parenthood Los Angeles. She has been writing poetry since 2015. Her poems have been published in *Halfway Down the Stairs, Moon Magazine*, and *The Jewish Journal*. Her work was recently published in *Constellations*, an annual print literary journal.

"My father was a West Point graduate who won a Bronze Star for his service in Korea. Watching him struggle with dementia at the end of his life called up military imagery—life a battlefield we're all trying to survive with dignity and honor."

R. Bratten Weiss *Over by the Coliseum*

R. Bratten Weiss is the author of *Mud Woman*, a collaborative chapbook with Joanna Penn Cooper (Dancing Girl Press, 2018). Her creative work has been published in *Two Hawks Quarterly, The Cerurove, Lycan Valley Press Publications, Figroot Press, Jesus the Imagination, Convivium, US Catholic, Poetry Pacific, Connecticut River Review, Ethel Zine*, and *On the Seawall*. She is a Pushcart and Best of the Net nominee.

Rosaleen Bertolino *Two Birds*

Rosaleen Bertolino was born and raised in the San Francisco Bay Area and received her MA in Creative Writing from San Francisco State University. Her fiction has appeared in *The New England Review, Vassar Review, Storyscape, Superstition Review, failbetter, Orca*, and many other fine publications. Currently living in Mexico, she is the founder and host of Prose Café, a monthly reading series based in San Miguel de Allende. Her debut story collection, *The Paper Demon & Other Stories* is forthcoming from New Rivers Press in 2021.

"It took me a long time, years and years, to find my way into this story. At first, I was too protective of this character, who, despite her cunning and intelligence, leads a life of involuntary innocence. At last, one day, the little bird appeared and tunneled straight into Alice's heart."

Rose M. Smith *Pressure Point*

Rose M. Smith has appeared in such publications as *Main Street Rag, The Iconoclast, Pedestal Magazine, Pavement Saw, Pud-*

ding Magazine, Concrete Wolf, and other journals, as well as several anthologies. Rose is an Associate Editor at Pudding House Publications, author of *Shooting the Strays* (Pavement Saw Press, 2003) and *A Woman You Know* (Pudding House Publications, 2005), co-editor of *Cap City Poets: Columbus and Central Ohio's Best Known, Read, and Requested Poets* (Pudding House Publications, 2008), and is a 2010 inductee into *Pudding House's Poets Greatest Hits* collection.

R.R Shepard *Turn Your Feelings into Animals and Talk to Them*

R.R Shepard is a writer, classicist, and entrepreneur. Shepard has published fiction, nonfiction, poetry, and translations, most recently in *The Mystery Tribune, Archer*, and *Amarillo Bay*. Based out of nowhere in particular, Shepard is currently co-founding a philosophy start-up called Invisible and working on (hopefully) the final draft of a novel. Thoughts, etymologies, and more information can be found at rrshepard.com.

"In August of 2018, I moved to New Mexico, recently engaged, to begin my MFA in fiction. While I was packing up to leave, I was half-listening to a Radiolab podcast, and between running from room to room tracking down socks and ski gear, I heard the story of a woman intervening in a bull attack somewhere in the middle of nowhere. I didn't think much of it, or note down any of the details, but the image stuck. A few weeks later, I had moved to a small town in the mountains outside of Albuquerque, and I was given the prompt for my first fiction class to read Alice Munro's 'Passion' and use the idea of passion as a springboard exercise into a short story. 'Turn Your Feelings into Animals and Talk to Them' was what came out, in one fell swoop. I showed up to that first class without much of an opinion on the piece. What ended up giving meaning to the piece was someone else; an Australian woman in the program who I ended up falling in love with and leaving my fiancé for. Months later, in the throes of romance, she told me it was her favorite piece of mine, and that after I'd read it in class, she walked home crying. She also informed me to cut the last two lines, which I did. This remains the only change to the piece. She remains my best reader."

Ryan Havely *How to Be Alive*

Ryan Havely earned his first degree from Ohio University and his last from Minnesota State.

"I honestly don't remember. My wife was asleep three floors above me and I had to write something or I wouldn't value my life."

Sage *The Prophet Bathes in Styx*

Sage Sage holds an MFA in Creative Writing from St. Mary's College of California. Their work appears in *Empty Mirror, North American Review, Penn Review, The Rumpus*, and elsewhere.

"'The Prophet Bathes In Styx' came out of a craft workshop with poet Tongo Eisen-Martin. The poem lies at the intersection of a few complicated ideas I have been trying to write towards, namely the influence of my gender identity on my sexuality and vice versa; the quiet rage of inadequacy queer people can feel within cis-heteronormative standards of love and desire; and what we give up, willingly or not, to be with someone who may even return our efforts and devotion."

Sharon Charde *Not*

Sharon Charde, a retired psychotherapist and a writing teacher since 1992, has won numerous poetry awards, the latest being 2018 finalist in the Blue Light Press chapbook contest for *Unhinged* to be published in 2019, Sixty Four Best Poets of 2018 by *The Halcyone*, and semi-finalist in the 2019 Grid contest for full-length collections for *The Glass Is Already Broken,* to be published by Blue Light Press in 2021. She is published over eighty times In journals and anthologies of poetry and prose, including *Calyx, Mudfish, The Paterson Review, Ping Pong, Rattle, Poet Lore, Upstreet* and *The Comstock Review,* and has had seven Pushcart nominations. She has also edited and published *I Am Not A Juvenile Delinquent*, containing the work of the adjudicated teenaged females she has volunteered with since 1999 at a residential treatment center in Litchfield Ct. A memoir with the same title, about her work with the girls, was published by Mango Publishing in June 2020 to much positive response. She has three first prize-winning chapbooks, *Bad Girl At*

The Altar Rail, Four Trees Down From Ponte Sisto and *Incendiary* as well as a full-length collection, *Branch In His Hand,* published by Backwaters Press in November 2008, which was adapted as a radio play by the BBC, broadcast in 2012. *After Blue,* for which she won honorable mention in Finishing Line Press's 2013 chapbook contest, was published in September 2014. She has been awarded fellowships to the Vermont Studio Center, Virginia Center For The Creative Arts, The MacDowell Colony, The Ucross Foundation and The Corporation Of Yaddo.

Sharon J. Wishnow *Night Watch*

Sharon J. Wishnow is a Massachusetts native who made her way to Northern Virginia via the Netherlands. As a fiction writer, Sharon is deeply interested in themes surrounding the environment, science, and society. She has an MFA from George Mason University and serves as a board member for the Women's Fiction Writers Association. Learn more at her author site, www.sharon-wishnow.com.

"The character, Luke, with his penny-red fur, was inspired by the brave daughter of close friends. She sadly lost her battle with leukemia, but her memory and their love continue to fill the world with hope for a cure."

Susan Cummins Miller *Genesis*

Tucson writer/geologist **Susan Cummins Miller's** award-winning poems, short stories, and essays have appeared in numerous journals and anthologies, including *What We Talk About When We Talk About It: Vol. I, What Wildness Is This: Women Write about the Southwest, And All Our Yesterdays, More Voices of New Mexico, SandScript,* and *Roundup! Great Stories of the West from Today's Leading Western Writers.* She compiled and edited *A Sweet, Separate Intimacy: Women Writers of the American Frontier, 1800-1922,* and pens the *Frankie MacFarlane, Geologist,* mysteries.

"A memory of a geologic field trip to the Great Basin inspired 'Genesis.'"

Susan Kress *Sisterhood*

Susan Kress was born and educated in England and now resides in Saratoga Springs, New York, after a long career teaching at Skidmore College. She has poems published in *Salmagundi, New Letters, La Presa, Halfway Down the Stairs, Passager, 3Elements Review*, and other journals.

"'Sisterhood' is a playful poem about a girl's surprising introduction to her sexual life. The epigraph is, of course, invented."

Sylvia Maultash Warsh *The German Credit*

Sylvia Maultash Warsh is the author of the *Dr. Rebecca Temple* mystery series, one of which, *Find Me Again*, won an Edgar. Her historical novel, *The Queen of Unforgetting*, was chosen by Project Bookmark Canada for a plaque installation. She has had a novella and many short stories published, four of which have been nominated for major awards. She's currently working on an historical novel with paranormal elements set in 1840s Washington, DC. She also teaches writing to seniors.

"My parents were incarcerated in labour camps by the Germans in World War Two. I grew up listening to my mother's experiences during those years, which left an indelible mark on me. In high school, I took German from a teacher who looked down on his students, an odd-looking little man with stiff posture, ruddy skin, and a Hitler-like moustache. I couldn't watch him in class without wondering what he had done in the war. He was the basis of the teacher in my story."

Taunja Thomson *Carnival Evoning*

Taunja Thomson's poetry has also appeared in *Potomac* and *Surreal Poetics*.

William Derge *No Tugging Today*

William Derge won the $1,000 2010 Knightsbridge Prize judged by Donald Hall and the Rainmaker Award judged by Marge Piercy. He has received honorable mentions in contests sponsored by

The Bridge, Sow's Ear, and *New Millennium*, among others. He has been awarded a grant by the Maryland State Arts Council.
Woody Woodger *Skeleton Flower*

Woody Woodger is a trans, pan, anarcho-commie currently living in Washington, DC. Her poetry has appeared, or is forthcoming, from *DIAGRAM, Northern New England Review, Drunk Monkeys, RFD, Exposition Review, peculiar,* and *Rock and Sling,* and has been nominated for *Best of the Net.* Her first chapbook, *postcards from glasshouse drive* (Finishing Line Press) has been nominated for the 2018 Massachusetts Book Awards. You can find her bi-week column Pre-Op Thot on COUNTERCLOCK Magazine where she serves as Blog Editor and Poetry Reader. If THAT wasn't enough (and it was) you can find her on Instagram and Twitter @lovlyno1.

"This poem is so special to me because it's true. 'You can see them down to their veins. / You're like that, she says. Imagine / how beautiful you are to be like that.' That was an actual text a friend of mine sent me when I was doubting if the abuse actually happened. My partner had treated me terribly, continuously, and by their own admission in the relationship. But when they broke up with me, they proceeded to dox me on social media as an abuser. Whether intentionally or not, they used this as a way to continue to control me and silence me. This happens with alarming regularity to trans women and thankfully many in my social circle did not believe this person based on their behavior and their intimate knowledge of the relationship. I asked my friend why I was so vulnerable to these people. This was not the first abusive relationship I experienced. So my friend told me about the skeleton flower, this delicate thing that will show its veins in the first rain. She said this as if it were a special gift. I'll never be able to repay her for that."

Edited
By
Susannah
Carlson
&
Shelley
Valdez
What We Talk About When we Talk About It
Variations
on the Theme
of Love
VOLUME
1

Another title in the Darkhouse Books Riff series

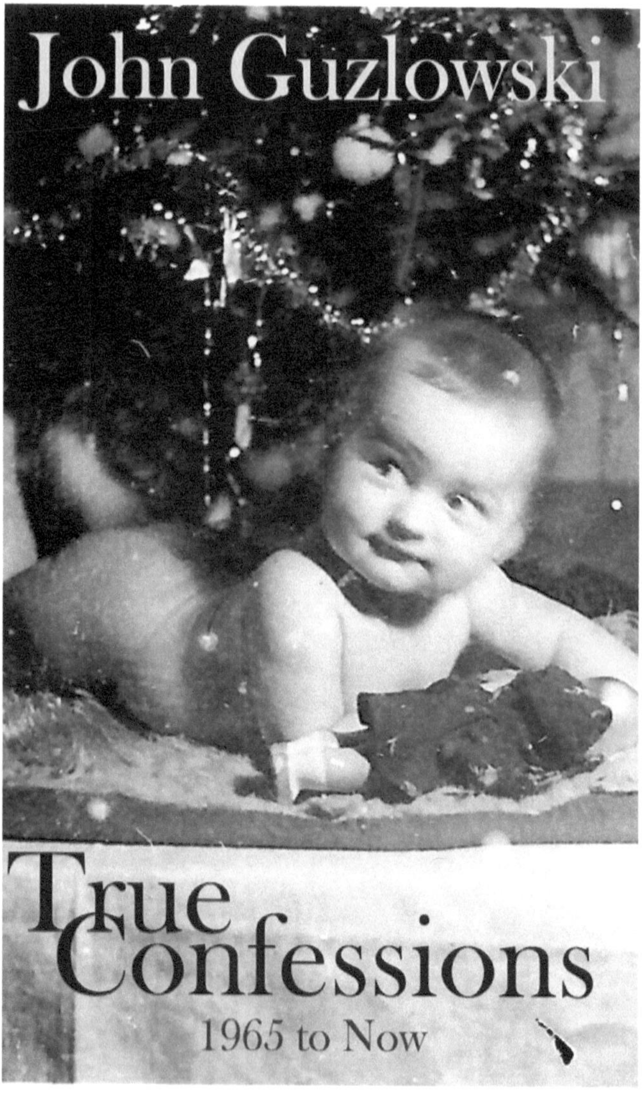

About This Book

The typeface in this book is 11.5 Garamond and Helvetica. The title font is Black Chancery. It was laid out using Adobe InDesign software and converted to PDF for uploading to the printing facility.

About Darkhouse Books

Darkhouse Books is dedicated to publishing literary, mystery, science-fiction, and horror.

Darkhouse Books is located in Niles, California, an inadvertently
preserved, 120 year old, one-sided railtown, forty miles from San Francisco. Further information may be obtained by visiting our website at www.darkhousebooks.com.